# SLEEP WITH ANGELS

## LORENE J. HUMPAL

TitleTown
PUBLISHING

Copyright © 2014 by Lorene Humpal

FIRST EDITION

Library of Congress Cataloging-in-Publication Data On File

For inquiries about volume orders, please contact:
TitleTown Publishing, LLC
PO Box 12093
Green Bay, WI 54307-12093
920-737-8051

Published in the United States by TitleTown Publishing
*http://www.titletownpublishing.com*

Distributed by Midpoint Trade Books
*www.midpointtrade.com*

Printed in the United States of America

Interior design by Vally Sharpe
Cover Design by Michael Short

# DEDICATION

*To my husband, Richard M. Humpal, whose love, patience, and understanding made it possible for me to write this book. He has been through it all with me, the good and—mostly—the bad. I dedicate this book to Richard with all my love.*

*It was God who armed us with strength and made our way possible. Without Him, I would not have been able to finish this journey. He was with us every day—perpetually, uniformly, and on every occasion.*

*Richard and my faith helped me persevere.*

## AUTHOR'S NOTE

This is a true story. I spent many years searching for the truth, and my investigations led me in many directions, as I tried to understand all sides of the story. I searched every record and interviewed many, many people. During most of the journey, I was scared to death for my safety and that of my husband and sons.

# FOREWORD

Lorene Humpal and her husband Richard were among the leaders of St. Timothy Lutheran Church who asked me to serve as their pastor and helped me and my family move into our new home in Edmonds, Washington. That was September 10, 2001.

Later we were all struggling to come up with a good answer to the question, "Why does God let bad things happen to good people?" Sometimes the bad things are caused by the selfish choices people make, as when terrorist choose to fly into buildings. Sometimes there seems to be no explanation. And when bad things do take place in our lives, how is it some people are able to survive them and even thrive in the aftermath?

Lorene's story may point to some answers to this second question: a God who loves us, who brings loving people into our lives to support and encourage us. And I would suggest that this then leads us closer to our first question. Perhaps God allows pain to touch us so we cannot turn a blind eye to the fact that the world in which we find ourselves is somehow not what it should be. There is selfishness and there is death. But there is also life and hope of goodness. There is music and forgiveness. I hope that God will allow Lorene's story to touch you so that you may see more clearly the one who turns sorrow into joy.

*Michael Schuessler*
*March 9, 2014*

*Sleep with Angels* will keep you on the edge of your seat, as Lorene Humpal unravels secrets of her past.

We met Lorene years ago. She is a highly talented church organist with a passion for music and a strong faith and devotion to God. Her buoyant outlook, quick wit, and stubborn Irish tenacity have allowed her to overcome life's hurdles with seeming ease. What a good thing that is, as one day Lorene shared with us a dark secret surrounding the story of her birth.

Now she is ready to share that story with the world. The fact that Lorene is alive today to tell the story is, in itself, a miracle. God truly watched over and protected his special creations. When we experience terrifying or perhaps tragic events that are sadly a part of the world we live in today, we need to take notice that God's love for us is never failing. He is always by our side. Like Lorene, we need to hold tight to God so that we too can triumph and be a light and a joy to those around us.

*Gail and Bob McCaughey*
*March 15, 2014*

# SLEEP WITH ANGELS

# PART 1

## LONELY STREET

1

# Hell

The people of Minneapolis swore that they had died and gone to hell. The black moonless night was sweltering and humid, with only a faint breeze. The sidewalks were sweating right along with the people, who wilted in the hot, fetid air. As the night burned into the early morning hours of Monday, July 27, 1936, a fifteen year-old girl named Margaret Bolin went into labor, two weeks shy of a full-term pregnancy. She felt as if the night would never end. By two o'clock in the morning, her entire household was in an uproar.

Margaret's father rushed out into the night, walking two blocks through the shabby neighborhood. Finally, he reached the pay phone and called the hospital for an ambulance, then headed back through the streets of run-down rentals to their simple white clapboard building. The Bolins could not afford to own a home, so they rented the second-floor apartment, where Margaret's mother—who was thirty-eight and pregnant herself—tried to care for her moaning daughter.

The Dog Star, which rises and sets in late July and August, shone in the sky as the city endured the worst dog days in history. The heat had started in June, bringing record high temperatures to much of the United States. Minnesota was not immune. The summer of 1936 still holds all records for heat.

With no refuge from the heat, a great drought dehydrated the nation's heartland, creating the Dust Bowl, and turning the Land of 10,000 Lakes into a sauna. Minnesota's woodland turned to tinder, and forest fires blazed across hundreds of square miles. The corn shriveled in farmers' fields, and thirsty grasshoppers sucked moisture from farm animals' eyeballs. One week, in Minneapolis alone, a record 377 people died, and many of the deaths were blamed on the heat. Though home air-conditioning had been available since 1932, few could afford it, so the only relief for most people came from a cool drink or the steady hum of a fan. Many people resorted to sleeping in parks, even if they had homes.

Margaret's five younger brothers and sisters were afraid and crying. The commotion was too much for all of them. While Margaret was in the throes of labor, the family of eight, crammed into the roasting two-bedroom apartment, was panicked. Margaret was miserable, aware that she was paying the price for what she'd done.

At two-thirty in the morning, Minneapolis General Hospital dispatched an ambulance to the Bolin house, just a few blocks away. Rigid and sweating in labor, Margaret moaned and tossed. Still, she noticed the two attendants' knowing looks when they saw her age and condition. She had seen the same looks on the faces of neighborhood men and women, who had long glared at her while gossiping that she was an out-of-control tramp.

With sweat dripping down their faces, the attendants carried Margaret away from her screaming sisters and brothers, down the long stairs from the second floor, while she complained about the bumpy ride down the stairs and out into the night. The neighbors were out on their lawns, watching the attendants put the writhing girl into the ambulance in the sweltering night. They didn't miss a thing.

Bert and Barbara Bolin decided to stay home to calm their other children and each other. "What are we going to do?" Barbara cried.

Bert was also crying, as he didn't know how to answer his wife. They were all-too-aware that they had no money and no future. All they had was a fifteen-year-old daughter who pushed them to the brink of hopelessness.

Both of them had spoiled Margaret, but Bert was especially good at it, always calling Margaret his "Little Beauty." He had been a sheet-metal worker but, thanks to their drinking, the Bolin parents had always been poor, even before the Great Depression. Once the Depression hit in 1933, one third of America's workforce was unemployed, and those fortunate enough to have jobs had seen their wages fall by forty percent. Many people worked for the Works Progress Administration (WPA), a jobs-creation program which Franklin Delano Roosevelt had started the year before. The WPA didn't pay much—thirty dollars per month—but it was better than nothing. Many of the worst-off Americans resorted to picking apples or other fruit from random trees and selling the fruit for a few cents on street corners. Those who could afford to go out to eat at a local diner would always order the "blue plate special," the cheapest thing on the menu. But many others relied on the charity of their neighbors, often showing up at the back doors of homes, looking for a meal or even a scrap of food.

Unable to find work in his trade, Bert Bolin worked for the WPA. At the age of forty, he could barely support his family in the uncomfortable, ramshackle apartment in their ratty South Minneapolis neighborhood. The money he brought in was hardly enough to keep the large family fed and clothed, but they got by. At least, the family did. Margaret was another story.

A starry-eyed girl, Margaret was fourteen in 1934 when the first Thin Man movie came out, and she quickly came to idolize Myrna Loy in all her silver-screen glory. The glamorous actress played opposite William Powell in *The Thin Man*, and together, the pair created "Nick and Nora Charles," an elegant New York City couple who lived a delightful life of leisure in several films. Nora Charles wore silk lingerie as she lounged around all day, then drank martinis all night, wearing perfect gowns and glittering gems under luxurious fur coats.

For Margaret, as beautiful as she was young, the Nora Charles lifestyle came alive on the big screen. Thanks to many years of her father's fawning, the girl felt that, because she was so beautiful, she deserved such a life, that she could—and should—have all of the glamour, elegance, and leisure of Nora Charles. Reading magazines about real socialites who lived like Nora Charles, Margaret pictured herself living with an elegant and handsome husband who doted on her and poured her exotic cocktails while she pranced around in silk lingerie.

Though such fantasies were well beyond the reach of a young Irish girl in the middle of a desperate depression, Margaret felt that she deserved to turn such a fantasy into a reality. After all, despite her family's poverty, Margaret grew up with a strong sense of entitlement, born from her father's attentions—and those of other males. She had developed a cunning instinct about the opposite sex and their interest in her, and she was quite young when she realized that she could live the lovely life that she believed she deserved, thanks to the largesse of wealthy men. By the age of fourteen, this had become her goal.

Other than her father's praise for her beauty, Margaret had other reasons to believe that her looks would shower her with rewards. In 1934, at the age of thirteen, she had won a Minneapolis beauty contest at the Radio City Theater. Though that was only a local contest, not big enough to give her the notoriety that she craved, Margaret was still determined that her beauty would pay off. She would reap the rewards to which she was entitled.

With striking, sea-green eyes surrounded by a rose-petal complexion and black hair, Margaret was stunning. She liked to wear her favorite colors, red and lavender, which flattered her exotic-looking eyes. Even as a young woman, she had lush curves in all the right places—curves that men found irresistible. Margaret knew how to show them off, wearing her cotton dresses tight around the hips and with an extra button undone. With her coy body language, she was often rewarded by men who stopped to give her a second look.

Margaret lived in a time in which it was difficult to scrape together the money for a dime store lipstick, but her moral compass was shaped by her narcissism and materialism. Like many Americans who had fallen in love with the likes of Bonnie and Clyde, Pretty Boy Floyd, and Al Capone, Margaret shared some of their ethical orientation. And while most people realized that the ritzy lifestyles of the elite were extravagant beyond fantasy, Margaret read the society pages and studied America's privileged few—the Rockefellers and Kennedys, the Melons and Bechtels. In her mind, she courted the males of such families, pining for the ease and comforts of their lovely lives. She would avoid her parents' stark poverty by taking advantage of her considerable, though superficial, assets.

Even when she was younger, Margaret enjoyed showing off her figure. At age twelve, she always wore bright red lipstick—the reddest she could buy at the dime store—and she painted her toenails with bright red polish, showing them off in open-toed sandals. The girl had a habit of judging people by the only two characteristics that mattered to her: looks and money. As she matured from childhood into adolescence, Margaret maintained this solid sense of what was important in life.

Margaret was an extremely good liar. Lying made her feel invincible and she seemed to have practiced it, honing her deceptive nature and skills as her own art form. Before long, beguilement became part of her character, her human essence. But her technique was flawed: Margaret tended to emphasize the truthfulness of her statements, which destroyed her credibility. With an early and devout admiration of herself, she was also narcissistic—a trait that she would have all of her life. But as an adolescent, Margaret's overconfidence convinced her that she was well above society's rules.

Margaret's black hair and beautiful green eyes came from her mother, Barbara, who was Irish. Barbara had a quick wit and a good sense of humor, and she liked to have a good time. Barbara often said that she could never look at another man, since she had married the best—a sentiment that others agreed with. Tall and slim, Bert was a graceful dance partner, who would take his wife out ballroom dancing whenever they could. Though Barbara wore the affordable cotton dresses that were the style of the day, the couple won ballroom dancing contests.

Barbara and Bert really wanted only one child, but by 1936, Margaret was the oldest of six. Still, the Bolins enjoyed going out to have good times without the children, so they often left Margaret at home babysitting. When the coast was clear, however, Margaret would slip outside to meet a boy who was sitting in his car, parked down the street from her house, waiting for her.

It wasn't easy on her younger brothers and sisters to fend for themselves while their older sister went out for her own good times. As the boys plied her with alcohol and pawed at her curves, Margaret realized the value of all that she had to offer.

When she was thirteen, Margaret got into real trouble. She met a man named Kenneth Warren, who had a job and, more to the point, he had money. He would buy Margaret a good meal and maybe take her to a movie or buy her a small bottle of Radio Girl perfume, the cheap dime-store brand that was popular because it was affordable. Margaret had developed quite a taste for beer and cigarettes, and she would do anything for a man who would feed her vices or ply her with other gifts. Though most of the gifts that she received were not expensive, 13-year-old Margaret would give men sex in exchange for their trinkets and booze. The relationship between Margaret and Kenneth Warren was no different.

Except this time, her parents caught them.

Mr. and Mrs. Bolin took their daughter to Minneapolis General Hospital and had her examined by a doctor. Tests seemed to show that she was not pregnant, but hospital officials made Margaret divulge the name of the man. When she told them, the police arrested him. Warren was prosecuted and put on probation for statutory rape of a minor, while Margaret was put on "probation counseling."

It didn't work. By the time she was fourteen, she broke probation by keeping late hours, smoking, and drinking. Like her parents, Margaret liked alcohol and she enjoyed partying with friends. She brought friends to Medicine Lake, a short distance outside of Minneapolis, where Minnesotans had cabins and summer homes. There, the girl broke in to her aunt's cottage, where she had wild parties with her friends, including some boys, of course.

Margaret got caught, again.

Because she had broken her probation, Margaret was sentenced to six months at the Sauk Center Training School for Delinquent Girls. Praying that she wasn't pregnant, she started serving her sentence on January 28, 1935. When Margaret was paroled six months later, she was surrounded by rampant rumors that she had given birth to a baby boy, whom her parents were raising as their own. This rumor, supposedly substantiated by hospital records, asserted that her parents had agreed to raise the baby as their own, but that they absolutely would not raise another baby after that one.

At fifteen, Margaret drank at beer halls and went to hotels with men who were seventeen to twenty years old, giving them sex in exchange for whatever she could get in return. While she liked men, sex, and gifts, she probably did not consider herself a prostitute. Rather, she was a promiscuous girl without a conscience, she was greedy, and she wanted to find a rich young man who appreciated what she had to offer so that she could get away from her family.

She hated babysitting her brothers and sisters and didn't want to help her mother around the house all the time. And, like most people during the Depression, she wanted to be rich. Desperate to marry a rich man so she could live the Nora Charles life of luxury, she thought that her strategy should at least help her catch a man who had a job so that she could escape poverty.

Margaret never understood that men and boys used her for their own pleasures, just as she used them. She was too young and naïve to realize that the trades were fully consummated, that her men did not feel that they owed her anything further. Since she put out so easily for a small gift, such men might come back for more, but not for what Margaret wanted. They would give her money and gifts and tell her how beautiful she was, but rich men who take pretty poor girls to beer halls and hotels don't have marriage on their minds. Men like that see sophisticated rich women as suitable for marriage, but pretty poor girls are only toys, for fun. Margaret had no idea. She coveted everything that rich people had and thought that she deserved it because of her beauty, because her father had told her so. When Margaret attended Jackson Grade School, she found that she was far more mature than the other girls her age, and she had nothing in common with them. Since school was not for her, Margaret had little education after grade school, other than the education she received on the streets and at the reformatory.

Barbara knew that her eldest daughter didn't have a lick of sense, and she begged Margaret to change her ways. Barbara saw that the girl was selfish and materialistic, wanting the luxuries of riches, and that Margaret lied to shield herself from her parents' scolding.

But Bert and Barbara could do nothing with their daughter. Four months after she was paroled from the Sauk Center, Margaret was pregnant. She was fifteen years old, and her mistakes were only beginning.

# 2

## July 27th

Lying frightened in the ambulance, Margaret felt the sweat streaming down her face and mixing with her tears. With little sympathy for a fifteen-year-old girl who was ready to deliver a baby, the attending doctor hardly paid attention to Margaret, telling the ambulance driver to step on it. The driver sped away from the house with sirens whining all the way to the hospital. With no open windows in the back of the ambulance, Margaret could not bear the heavy air. She was screaming when the car pulled up to the hospital's emergency room entrance. By then, the ambulance team was eager to get her into the hospital so they could be done with her.

At that time, the downtown area had not yet reached the hospital complex, which was surrounded by wood-framed houses and quaint mom-and-pop businesses. The large Minneapolis General Hospital towered over the older neighborhood. Separate buildings housed the nursing school and nurses' dormitory, which were connected by tunnels to the seven-story hospital building. The facility covered a full city block. The hospital itself was built on granite floors, which made the building feel cool, at least at first. The hospital did not have air-conditioning, and its hot interior was filled with a medicinal smell.

On the third floor, hanging lights loomed overhead and illuminated the stark white walls, while maternity nurses dripped with sweat as they wrapped mothers and babies in ether-soaked cloth, trying to bring down their internal temperatures. When the elevator doors opened for Margaret and her attendants, the maternity department staff immediately admitted her into a labor room.

Working efficiently, the nurses dressed the girl in a starched gown, took her vital signs, measured her stage of dilation, and then they gave her an enema. For Margaret, that was the worst part so far—an enema on top of the horrible, grinding labor pains—and it was almost more than she could bear. In the final preparation for the coming birth, an attendant who wasn't very experienced dripped sweat on Margaret as he shaved her private parts.

A labor-room nurse came and kept a close eye on Margaret as the minutes burned away.

Margaret's pains came closer together and by three o'clock in the morning the labor nurse knew that it was time. Dilation was complete and the girl's pains were continuous, an unrelenting tumult that Margaret could hardly comprehend. The nurse gave the order and Margaret was quickly wheeled into the delivery room. Screaming and moaning, she was transferred onto the delivery table, where she was strapped down with her legs wide apart and her feet high in the stirrups.

Though the nurses at Minneapolis General Hospital dealt with thousands of women in labor, they felt unusual pity and tenderness for the young girl who was so tiny, so vulnerable. With the face of a movie star, Margaret was only about five-foot-two and fine-boned, weighing about one-hundred-forty pounds at full term. Before she had become pregnant, Margaret had a good figure, with nice curves on her one-hundred-ten-pound frame. It bothered her that she had gained weight with her pregnancy and she was angry at the baby for doing that to her.

"Too bad her man can't have this baby," muttered the older nurse, Edna Kaltenberg, who had seen had a lot. "It'll be over soon, honey," whispered another nurse, bending down to gently wipe tears and sweat from Margaret's face. "Be a brave girl."

Margaret didn't care what they said. She wanted the baby out!

The delivery room door swung open and a doctor entered. Large sweat circles stained the underarms of his rumpled white coat. "It's too hot and I'm too tired to go through all the pushing business," Doctor Harrington declared. "Give her gas and let's get that baby out of there."

Unprepared, Margaret's eyes rolled in agony and fear as one of the nurses strapped a mask over her face. "Breathe in deeply," the nurse instructed her.

Soon, Margaret's body went limp. Mercifully, she was unconscious.

Holding a tiny head in his hands, Doctor Harrington used his foot to pull a stool over to the delivery table so that he could sit down to deliver the baby. He guided first one shoulder and then the other, and then, with one last contraction, the rest of the baby was born at nineteen minutes after three.

"When did little girls start having babies?" asked the doctor. No one answered.

They all knew that good girls knew nothing of sex. Good girls did not want to know. At least, that's what good girls said. Certainly, they did not participate in sex until their wedding nights and then, preferably, with a becoming reluctance. Schools, of course, did not teach about sexuality or reproduction, coming closest when they held intimate little talks—with boys and girls appropriately separated—about the pistils and stamens of flowers.

Leaving Doctor Harrington to finish delivering the placenta and sew up the mother, the blonde nurses carried the black-haired newborn girl to a nearby table. Like her mother, the baby was beautiful, with green eyes and a peaches-and-cream complexion. Though she was two weeks premature, the baby was very healthy at six pounds two ounces.

The nurses slapped the newborn's back, making her cry, and then they wiped her off and dropped a one-percent solution of silver nitrate into her eyes, since she was two weeks premature. They wrote the mother's name, the birth date, and the time on a wide, sticky piece of adhesive tape, which they fastened to the infant's back, between her tiny shoulder blades. Then they diapered the baby, wrapped her in a receiving blanket, and carried her into the nursery, where they bedded her down next to the seventy other newborns who slept and cried under the watchful supervision of Ella Englestad. Doctor Harrington, along with Doctor B.W. Ureun, signed the infant's birth certificate.

After the exhaustion of giving birth and the effects of the gas, Margaret slept for a few hours, until the sunrise began sparkling golden light on the city of Minneapolis. Though her life had caught up with her, the young mother planned to get back to the boys and beer halls again, as soon as she could get out of the hospital and get rid of the baby. Margaret did not know that she would not be going home now that her baby was born.

Without even asking to see her baby, Margaret named the infant Shirley Ann, after the matinee idol, Shirley Temple. The child star became famous at the age of four, when she starred in her first movie, and she was the top box-office draw throughout the mid1930s. Every mother took her little daughters to see Shirley Temple, who sang and danced in the movies. For Margaret, that name was likely the only one that she could think of quickly. Indeed, in 1936, "Shirley" was the second most popular name for a girl, after "Mary." At home, Margaret's father paced the floor while her mother soothed the other children, who eventually went back to sleep. Barbara remained restless. The extreme heat and the night's uproar had caused such an upheaval that the Bolins were unable to sleep. Finally, Bert again walked the two blocks to the pay phone and called General Hospital, asking about his daughter. He learned that Margaret had given birth to a baby girl and that she was sleeping. Bert dashed back home to tell Barbara.

Though they were relieved by the news, the hopelessness of the situation weighed on their minds. Three months pregnant herself, Barbara worried about Margaret's baby. Bert only made thirty dollars a month working for the WPA. Who would take care of the baby? Who would pay for her clothes and her food? Where would she sleep? Other than the practicalities of survival and how to handle all of the complications and burdens of daily life, Margaret's parents had little interest in their first grandchild, who was born while they were still making babies themselves.

For families like the Bolins, the Great Depression had heaped anguish upon misery in the midst of their otherwise desperate lives. Thanks to their own drinking and all of their babies, Bert and Barbara were already poor. They had never owned their own home, and lived in a time when the Depression turned homeowners into renters and renters into desperate survivors. Children even played a game called "Eviction," moving dolls around as they pretended that they had been evicted. Oblivious and indifferent to the miserable realities for masses of people, rich men who held public office believed that the nation's social systems worked just fine.

Like many people around them, the Bolins felt defeated. Their parents were dead. Their living relatives were either in Ireland, too far away to be any help to the couple and their children, or they frowned on Bert and Barbara's lifestyle and would have nothing to do with them. As a result, the couple had no one to whom they could turn for assistance. And, while Margaret certainly would have benefited from a religious upbringing, her parents did not practice any formal religion. Though Barbara's family was Irish Catholic and Bert's was Protestant, and though they were good people, they were not religious. They had not had any of their children baptized. Without the support of relatives or a religious community, the family of eight simply survived their gloomy lives. Day after day, they put one foot in front of the other and trudged forward.

That was the life into which Shirley Ann Bolin was born on July 27, 1936.

# 3

## August 5th

It was perhaps a sign of the times that a 34-year-old woman seemed to have drowned herself in the Mississippi River, her ten-year-old son by her side. Holding the boy's hand, the woman said, "Let's go into the river." Jerking away from his mother, the boy said, "No." The woman put her purse on the bank of the river. "Take this," she said. "There's ten dollars in it." When the boy glanced at the purse on the bank, he heard a splash. When he turned back, his mother was gone.

A few miles away, in Minneapolis General Hospital, the maternity nurses watched over the crowded nursery and the young mothers on the ward. Minneapolis had many Swedish people—second only to Sweden—and most of the nurses in the unit were of Swedish descent. Edna Kaltenberg and Ruth Holtist worked under Ella Engletad, and all of them were blond-haired, blue-eyed young nurses who wore perfectly-ironed white starched uniforms. As straight-laced as they were nice looking, the women were sweet, dedicated, and very good at their jobs. Like grandmothers, the nurses cared for the new mothers on the ward, gently teaching each woman how to nurse her baby, and talking with them about what would happen in the coming days and weeks. The nurses loved all babies and each of them nurtured every precious newborn as if the infant were one of her own children. As the days passed, however, all of the nurses quickly became attached to a favorite infant, baby Shirley Ann.

A pretty baby with a precious Kewpie-doll curl on the top of her head, baby Shirley Ann especially captured the attention of the trio of nursery nurses. They spent a lot of time with her. Since the black-haired newborn was not very popular with her teenage mother, the nurses couldn't help but shower her with affection. They felt sorry for the fatherless child, whose mother—herself a child—showed no love for her own child. The girl in the bed seemed to care more for her mirror, lipstick, and magazines than she did about the infant, whose presence at feeding times appeared to be a nuisance. Since the teenager held and fed her baby for a short time, feeding her as quickly as possible, the nurses felt especially drawn to the pretty little baby. Whenever they could, they picked up baby Shirley Ann and showered her with affection. They swaddled her in tight, soft blankets, gave her hugs, and rested her on their bosoms as they walked with a gentle sway of their hips. When they could, they adorned her curly hair with tiny ribbons.

Alone in her room, Margaret endured the heat and discomforts of new motherhood—painful stitches and her milk coming in on the third day—by dreaming about beer parlors and good times. She lay in bed, resting on the side of her hip, with her blankets resting across her lap as she applied her bright red lipstick, brushed her hair, and read the society pages.

Perhaps as a ruse to get away from the other mothers and their babies, Margaret claimed to have a sore throat. In the days before antibiotics, doctors feared the spread of a bronchial infection throughout the maternity ward, so they moved Margaret out of the large unit and into a semi-private room, which was off by itself, located near a stairway out of sight of the nurse's station.

To protect infants, Minnesota law required that unwed mothers had to spend three months at a state-sponsored nursing home, where they would learn how to care for their newborns. But, before Margaret's baby was born, she already knew that she wanted to avoid going to the maternity home, so she thought that she would not keep the baby. The only reason she would have kept it was if she could get a rich boy to think he was the father, so that he would marry her. That was not in the cards, but Margaret tried anyway, scheming about her options. She had been with a few men and wanted the richest one to be the father, but she knew that she had to be careful. Still, the state had a deadline and Margaret knew that she had to act quickly.

Holding out hope that her unfortunate situation would lead to the perfect outcome—marriage to a rich boy—Margaret could not wait forever. She only had a few days. New mothers in the 1930s were considered invalids for nine days and, after that, the girl would have to give up the baby—and give up on the father—or go to the nursing home, which was the last thing Margaret wanted. She wanted her freedom, which did not include being saddled with a baby and it certainly did not include being locked up in a maternity home for three months.

Lying in the hospital, the hours passed slowly and the days ticked away, and the rich boy's marriage proposal did not come. Margaret decided not to keep her baby so that she could avoid going to the maternity home. As the state deadline loomed, she just wished that her baby would disappear.

Every time that the nurses brought the baby to Margaret for nursing, Margaret's eyes rolled. She obviously did not want to spend time nursing her baby, or doing anything else with her. At best, Margaret was pathetic at breastfeeding, quick to cut off the food and eager to send the baby back to the nursery. Still, the newborn seemed to be getting enough to eat, though just barely. With distaste for Margaret's attitude, the nurses seldom spoke to her. The teenage mother quickly lost their sympathy, as their hearts ached for her baby. In fact, whenever the nurses had little Shirley Ann in the nursery, they secretly gave her extra feedings of formula while they doted on the darling baby, who may as well have been an orphan.

It was still dark on the hot and quiet morning of Wednesday, August 5th, when a nurse brought the tiny infant to Margaret for her early-morning feeding. About twenty minutes later, a different nurse entered Margaret's room, lifted the sleeping baby from Margaret's side, and walked out without a word. The nurse wore a blue uniform and a gauze mask over her face. Always glad to give away the baby, Margaret thought nothing of a different nurse picking her up, since this had often happened in the nine days since she had delivered.

Soon, a third nurse walked into Margaret's room and approached the young woman's bedside. "Where's your baby?" the nurse asked.

"Back in the nursery," Margaret replied.

The nurse looked puzzled. "Who picked her up?"

"What difference does it make who picked Shirley Ann up?" Margaret shrugged, annoyed. "The nurse in blue picked her up!"

"What nurse in blue?" the nurse asked. "What did she look like?"

"Oh, I don't know," Margaret said. "I've never seen her before. She was just one of the nurses."

The nurse began to feel anxious and a little angry. "I'm here to get your baby!" she insisted.

"Well, she's not here," Margaret quickly retorted, eager to go back to sleep. "Can't you see that? The nurse in blue picked her up!"

The nurse ran out of the room and out of the hospital. She rushed across the street to the nurses' dormitory, where she woke up her supervisor, Ella Englestad. The Swedish charge nurse dressed quickly and then hurried across the street and up the two flights of stairs. When she arrived on the maternity unit, the duty nurses were waiting for her. Nurse Englestad ordered her staff to bring every baby from the nursery to each mother, immediately.

As the nurses began delivering the babies, the groggy mothers became bewildered. "What's wrong?" the mothers asked. "What does this mean? Are we supposed to feed our babies again? Is everything all right?"

Immediately, Ella Englestad knew that things were far from all right. The nurses had taken every baby to his or her mother and no babies were left. Margaret Bolin's nine-day-old infant was definitely missing. What could have happened to little Shirley Ann? Nurse Englestad called the superintendent of the hospital, Doctor C.E. Remy.

Doctor Remy listened intently. "Thank you, Nurse," he said. He was not about to fool around with this thing, whatever it was. He realized that Margaret Bolin's baby might have been kidnapped. If so, he doubted that the baby had been kidnapped for ransom, since the girl was obviously very young and poor. Besides, the public had been all-too-aware of the kidnapping of the Lindbergh baby and any potential kidnapper surely knew that kidnapping an infant would alert the FBI as well as the local police and, probably, the entire nation.

Doctor Remy wasted no time before calling the Minneapolis Police Department.

# 4

# A Nurse in Blue

The detective supervisor at the Minneapolis Police Department assigned a pair of detectives to the case. John Lehmeyer, fifty-seven years old, popped his straw hat onto his thinning hair, grabbed his jacket, and walked out of the police department with his partner, Harry Lindholm. Detectives Lehmeyer and Lindholm had a lot in common. Both were Swedish men in their late fifties, both were perfectionists, and both had been police chiefs before becoming detectives. They knew how to do their jobs as investigators and they worked well as a team.

They headed over to the hospital. Meanwhile, an officer at headquarters checked into the Bolin family and discovered that Margaret Bolin had been committed to the Sauk Center Training School for Delinquent Girls—and she was not the only one in the family who had served a sentence at the reformatory. The unwed mother's own mother, Barbara Bolin, had also done some time at the Sauk Center as a teenager. Also, Barbara's brother, John McDonough, had been in Red Wing, an institution for delinquent boys.

At five in the morning, when Lehmeyer and Lindholm arrived at Minneapolis General Hospital, they already knew about the family and about Margaret's juvenile delinquency. This led the detectives to initially suspect that someone in the family—possibly the young mother herself—was guilty. Discussing the case on the way to the hospital, they were suspicious of Margaret. "She's a player," they agreed. "That's for sure."

With the oppressive heat, the detectives did not put on their jackets, and the suspenders that held up their slacks showed over their white dress shirts. Walking quickly, Lehmeyer and Lindholm first called on Doctor Remy, the hospital's chief. A short, slight, bespectacled man with dark hair, Remy took his job seriously, running the hospital like a finely-tuned watch and demanding perfection from his nurses. When they were finished with Remy, the detectives asked the nurses a couple of quick questions before they turned their robust determination on Margaret.

Skilled detectives, they could tell if Margaret was telling the truth. Lehmeyer's bright blue eyes sparkled as he played the bad cop to Lindholm's good cop.

Despite all of their experience, they were not quite prepared for the young woman before them. Presenting a pleasant demeanor and a poker face, Lindholm blinked twice. His partner recognized the subtle signal that the detective found something disturbing—and it was obvious what it was.

Margaret laughed. She seemed to take the matter of her missing baby as a joke. She was calm as she told the detectives that, at about four-fifty-five in the morning, a nurse had come into her room to take the baby back to the nursery. Margaret said that the nurse wore a blue dress with a white apron and a mask over her mouth. This time, Margaret embellished her description of the blue-clad nurse, adding a description of the woman's shoes and noting the number of buttons on her dress. As if she couldn't care less about the detectives' questions, Margaret laughed throughout the interview, distracted as she adorned her lips with coats of bright red lipstick.

In fact, Margaret was relieved. The baby was gone and she assumed she would never have to see it again. And, in fact, Margaret was not worried about her baby because she did know what had happened to it.

The teenager, however, did not fool the two former police chiefs. The detectives knew that Margaret's frequent smiles revealed her insincerity, her averted gaze was one that liars always used, and her inappropriate laugh contradicted her innocence. Lehmeyer and Lindholm could tell that Margaret thought she knew how to handle police, and that she figured she could wrap them around her little finger because, after all, they were men and she was beautiful. Lehmeyer and Lindholm also assumed that she was guilty.

Still, the detectives had never met a young woman like Margaret. Why wasn't she panicked about the whereabouts of her baby? Instead, she actually seemed happy that Shirley Ann was gone. Considering her juvenile record, they doubted her story. In the eyes of the police, she was a criminal, implicated in some sort of plot to do away with her own baby.

The hospital, the police, and the media all had different theories of what happened to the baby. Doctor Remy said that there were no blue-clad nurses anywhere in Minneapolis General Hospital. After conducting a search of the hospital and its grounds, the police came up empty. The detectives investigated any means by which the infant could have been smuggled out of the complex. They checked a self-serve elevator, mainly used by nurses and doctors, which connected the hospital with the garage, where an attendant slept when he was off-duty. The attendant said that he had not heard any noises in the area.

The detectives also questioned Margaret's hospital roommate, a woman named Maude Wolfe. According to the detectives, Mrs. Wolfe had commented to one of the nurses that she "would like to have that infant." But the woman told Lehmeyer and Lindholm that she had been asleep during the early-morning comings and goings of Margaret's baby, and she had not noticed any nurse taking the baby. Mrs. Wolfe added, however, that whenever the lights were put on, Margaret insisted that they be turned off.

Throughout the day, rather than behaving seriously, Margaret continued to laugh, smile, and act carefree. Indeed, her narcissism seemed to border on mental illness. While she seemed to enjoy all of the attention directed at her, she also seemed to get a kick out of seeing how many lies the police would believe. She disgusted the detectives and nurses.

Margaret persisted in describing the nurse who took the baby as having worn a blue dress, but the detectives reasoned that, at that time of day—barely dawn, with only a feeble light trickling into the dark room—she could not have discerned the color of the dress. They also agreed that, as Margaret lay in bed, her line of vision would have been restricted to the upper portion of the nurse's body, so Margaret could not have seen the woman's shoes or counted the buttons, as she claimed.

As the morning warmed to afternoon, the detectives went to Margaret's neighborhood and questioned neighbors, some of whom had visited Margaret's mother, Barbara. The detectives asked the neighbors to keep an eye on the Bolin home, and to inform the police about any suspicious events or visitors. Then the investigators paid a visit to the Bolins themselves.

Since Barbara had a record, she was afraid of the police. Besides, the police were not exactly known as the good guys in those days. In any large city at that time, the police wielded great power, and this was especially the case in Minneapolis, a crime-ridden city where everything was corrupt. Engaged in ongoing wars with gangsters, the police were often corrupt—as corrupt as the mobsters they pursued. Home to the Minnesota Mafia, Minneapolis was as corrupt as the worst American cities of the 1930s and, since the police typically dealt with the most hardcore cases involving labor disputes, the effects of Prohibition, and gangsters, it was a rough time to be in trouble.

Barbara denied that she had visited Margaret the day before the baby disappeared, on Tuesday, August 4th, and claimed that she had not even left the house at all that day, except to walk a couple of blocks to the butcher shop on Cedar Avenue. Though the Bolin family lived within walking distance of the hospital, Barbara said that she had come right back home after going on her errand. Evasive as she answered the detectives' questions, she nonetheless admitted that she "didn't want that baby brought home!" The detectives left Mrs. Bolin inside the house and went out to the backyard to talk to her husband. When they asked Bert where his wife had gone on Tuesday afternoon, he told the detectives that Margaret had called, said that she was coming home on Wednesday, the fifth, and asked her mother to bring her some clothes. Barbara had gone to the hospital to see Margaret on August 4th.

When Barbara came out into the backyard, detectives Lehmeyer and Lindholm questioned her further. Finally, she admitted that she had gone to the hospital to see Margaret on the afternoon of the fourth. She said that she did not know why she had lied about that. While she was talking, Barbara claimed that she hadn't known that Margaret was pregnant until she went into labor. She also happened to add that a young Minneapolis man named Larry O'Reilly was the baby's father.

Radio broadcasters read the alarming news story on all of the local stations, telling a shocked community that a baby was missing from the hospital. Officials hoped that the news would generate leads about the baby's whereabouts from the community, but it generated more intrigue and fear than leads.

As the afternoon burned on, newsboys stood on street corners holding the evening paper high above their heads. "Extra! Extra!" they yelled. "Read all about it! Baby stolen from hospital!" Indeed, those were the exact words of the banner headline that ran across the front page of the *Minneapolis Journal* on the evening of Wednesday, August 5, 1936.

The story hit a raw nerve. Only four months earlier, Bruno Hauptmann had gone to the electric chair for kidnapping and killing the Lindbergh baby four years earlier, in 1932. That case had sensationalized the kidnapping of infants and aroused a horrified public that continued to buy newspapers. When baby Shirley Ann disappeared from the downtown Minneapolis hospital, the city's three competitive newspapers—the morning Tribune and its scrappier afternoon rivals, the *Journal* and the *Star*—covered every detail of the case, making the detectives' progress in the investigation common knowledge around kitchen tables throughout the greater Minneapolis area.

The wary public might have wondered if Hauptmann had been wrongfully executed. Could it be that he had not been the person who kidnapped the Lindbergh baby? Or was there suddenly another kidnapper out there who also preyed on newborns? The prospects were frightening, especially to those who lived in and around Minneapolis.

From the start, however, the Minneapolis story seemed vastly different from the Lindbergh case. On that first day, for example, the *Minneapolis Star* reported:

> *The girl mother was near exhaustion from constant police questioning. It was reported that she was hard boiled and cajoled with the police and kept on insisting that she wanted her baby back. She said that she wanted to find Shirley Ann, the name she had given her baby. They showed her the baby's empty crib, but she still told the same story about the nurse in blue taking her baby. She said that her parents had agreed to let her keep the baby, but they had not been to see her.*

The other newspapers picked up on the phrase "girl mother," which came to be the name by which Margaret was renowned in the local media. The press also described her as a "hard-boiled" juvenile delinquent and a teenager who had been around and who didn't care about anybody or anything. Providing the public with a clue as to the direction of the official inquiry, the Journal article reported that Doctor Remy felt that Margaret apparently had an outsider's help in smuggling the baby out of the hospital. Meanwhile, the media also shared that the police felt that the baby had been spirited away and kept at an out-of-the-way hiding place. The public was ordered to keep their eyes open for any clues that might lead to finding the baby alive.

Considering the evidence that they had already gathered, the detectives knew that Margaret was a "sport"—sexually active and promiscuous—because her juvenile records testified to the fact that she was a tramp. Besides, she always flirted with them, giving the police a good idea about what kind of girl she was.

Returning to the hospital, the detectives conducted an intensive second search of the building, from the attic to the basement. Officers checked every room, peeking into cupboards, laundry chutes, and toilet tanks—every little nook that could hide a small baby. They also re-checked the grounds, looking everywhere, but there was no sign of Shirley Ann.

Again and again, Margaret repeated the same story for the detectives. While she was at it, she flirted with them, winking and fluffing her hair as she glanced down at their chests and belts, or slightly twitching her lips and sighing as she looked not at their eyes but at their lips. Whether out of boredom or in a naïve attempt to manipulate the men, she relied as usual on her overt sexuality, which had never failed her on the streets of Minneapolis.

But detectives Lehmeyer and Lindholm were mature men, and they were not suckered by the child's adolescent attempts at flirting. After all, they were in their fifties, and Margaret was young enough to be among the youngest of their own children. If anything, her silly and ill-conceived behavior encouraged them to question her more in their effort to get her to slip up.

Unfortunately, Margaret was not just a good actress, but also a compulsive liar. No matter what the detectives' demeanor was, Margaret always smiled. She almost drove them crazy.

# 5

## LIPSTICK

With her baby gone, Margaret wanted to get on with her life. She was tired of the discomforts of new motherhood.

Her stitches itched and pulled on her private parts and, with no baby to nurse, milk filled her breasts and turned them into big, hard, aching knots. She was sick of the hot weather and, most of all, she was sick of being confined to General Hospital. She passed the time by reading the newspapers and listening to the news about herself on the radio, getting a kick out of her sudden celebrity status.

"Damn the Great Depression," Margaret thought, lying in bed for hours on end. "This Depression is not going to defeat me, and I will not become another beaten American, another luckless person selling apples on the street." While she spent her hours alone, Margaret was scheming, piecing together details of how she would name a rich man as the father of her missing baby. She knew that she would have to be cautious, to plan it just right, and it didn't help that the detectives had ordered a police matron to watch the girl like a hawk, day and night.

The matron watched as Margaret spent most of her time looking in her mirror and applying make-up and bright lipstick. The police matron felt that the detectives were dealing too gently with Margaret, who poured on the charm whenever the men were in range of her beautiful body.

The detectives labored through the heat to follow up on every lead and, on Thursday, they questioned Margaret yet again. Lindholm fingered his gold wedding band as Margaret dipped her chin and raised her eyelashes, looking into the investigator's bright eyes. Still, he continued to play the good cop while Lehmeyer grilled the girl. Before the Miranda Ruling, criminal justice systems in the 1930s largely ignored constitutional protections, and police often interrogated suspects harshly and endlessly before they would allow any attorneys to get involved.

The detectives also spoke again to Margaret's parents. They had learned that some people thought that Margaret's two-year-old brother was actually Margaret's child, and they had heard that the boy had been born at home. Under such circumstances, the police knew, birth certificates were less than reliable. Though they questioned Barbara and Bert about the boy, this line of inquiry remained fruitless.

The detectives were also suspicious of Margaret's cousin, Mrs. Clyde Peterson, who had once been a nurse at Minneapolis General Hospital. They felt that Mrs. Peterson would be familiar with the hospital entrances and exits, and would have been able to slip into the hospital and spirit away the baby.

The police had many unanswered questions, but they were sure about one thing: Margaret was guilty, an active participant in a plot that had resulted in the baby's disappearance. They felt certain that she was willing to get rid of her baby and that she had conspired to end the short life of baby Shirley Ann. Without a doubt, they believed, it was a case of infanticide. They understood that Margaret's baby would have been a burden on an already over-burdened family, that she did not want her baby, and believed that Margaret had done something to take care of her problem. Though they were working on this theory nonstop, they couldn't prove it. But, since the eyes of the entire nation were upon them, the detectives were anxious to solve the case.

They kept Margaret in the hospital so that they could keep her under surveillance, but the matron did not see everything that Margaret was up to. Sleeping late at night in Margaret's room, the matron missed it when Margaret slipped out into the dimly-lit hallway to visit with one of her boyfriends—Mike Osman—a teenage boy with slicked-back hair and bedroom eyes. With her hospital gown loosely covering her figure, Margaret leaned against the wall in the hospital corridor and flirted with the well-dressed young man.

# 6

## DIRECTIONS

Desperate for leads, the detectives read every personal ad in all three of the Minneapolis newspapers. Following up, they visited each of the newspapers and obtained all of the names and addresses of the people who had run the ads, and then they even visited every home related to the ads. Nothing proved to be related to Shirley Ann's disappearance.

The police interrogated Margaret for an hour one day and two hours the next. Trying to get her to slip up, they asked the same questions over and over. No matter how many times they asked her the questions, her demeanor remained flippant and facetious. Day in and day out, something else remained the same: Margaret's insistence that a nurse wearing blue had taken her baby.

As one day turned into the next, Margaret's name remained in the papers. She seemed to enjoy the attention. At streetcar stops and on every downtown comer, newspaper boys screamed the headlines.

"Extra! Extra! Read all about it!" yelled boys who were hawking the *Minneapolis Tribune.* "Baby believed to be dead!" Hungry to hear the news, the public bought all the papers available. Meanwhile, a young, cub reporter, Eric Sevareid, wrote that the police were seeking the missing baby's father, a young man named Larry O'Reilly.

Though O'Reilly lived with his parents in Minneapolis, he was not at home. According to his parents, the young man was participating in a Washington, D.C., dance marathon, a dance-until-you-drop contest for a cash prize, which had started on Wednesday, August 5th. He was expected to be in Washington for several days and then, following the contest, O'Reilly had planned to go to LaGrange, Illinois, where he would remain for weeks. His aunt lived there, running a mom-and-pop store known as Butler Place, and the young man intended to go there to do handyman jobs and whatever else his aunt needed him to do.

The detectives wondered if he had left town because he knew that he was the baby's father. They wondered whether the young man didn't want to be around when the baby was born. Or maybe there was more to his absence.

The police learned that O'Reilly's mother, in Minneapolis, had received a letter from her son, telling her how he was getting along. The letter was dated August 6, 1936. When the police inquired, the Irish-Catholic O'Reillys were shocked that their son had been named as the missing baby's father. His parents said that they did not even know Margaret Bolin. One of eight children in the very religious family, Larry had never given his parents any idea that he was in trouble.

The police made plans to have O'Reilly arrested in Illinois and extradited to Minneapolis, while they questioned the young man's best friend, who said that he had not seen Larry since the previous Saturday, August 1st, when he left for Washington, D.C., by bus.

The sweltering summer heat wave took its toll on the investigation. As the detectives went about the tedious work of questioning hundreds of people, they were burdened by the high temperatures and heavy humidity. The heat seemed to make everything more difficult. In addition, every industry in the city burned coal and, worse, the city was downwind from the Dakotas, which sent frequent dust storms into Minneapolis. When the dust wasn't blowing, the air was stagnant, unmoving. The city was rank with a humid odor of decay, and people could hardly breathe. Riding on a streetcar—even with open windows—was almost intolerable, as everyone in the crowded trolley seemed to exude body odor. To survive the heat, people flocked to the area lakes, though water levels were low and temperatures warm. People tried wrapping themselves in water-soaked sheets, only to have the sheets get warm and dank around their clammy bodies within a few minutes. Day in and day out, the relentless heat seemed to seethe from the streets and sidewalks as the sun beat down on Minnesota—and most of America.

Though Lehmeyer and Lindholm were weary from following every lead and questioning everyone related to Margaret Bolin, the detectives returned to the hospital to question the four nurses who worked on the maternity floor again. One by one, the nurses came forward and told the detectives of Margaret's indifference toward her child, confirming the detectives' suspicions of the young mother. On Friday, August 7th, the detectives retraced their steps, revisiting all the places they had been the day before and double-checking all of the information and statements they'd heard. Everything seemed to check out. And then, suddenly, momentum shifted.

A telephone call came in to the Superintendent of Minneapolis General Hospital. The sheriff of Rolla, North Dakota, called to report that a three-week-old baby with blue eyes had been abandoned in his town at one o'clock in the afternoon on July 29. According to the sheriff, the baby had been dropped off by a rather stout couple—a man with reddish-brown hair and a woman. They had been driving a 1933 or 1934 Chevrolet Coach with Goodyear-brand ribbed front tires and knobby-tread rear tires.

To the detectives, the lead sounded promising. They felt a surge of energy and renewed enthusiasm. Unfortunately, when they checked out the information, they decided that the North Dakota incident and baby were not related to their case.

Though the impoverished people of Minneapolis could not afford much during the Depression, at least newspapers were cheap. The daily papers cost three cents, while the Sunday paper was ten cents. With the daily news of the kidnapped baby and her girl mother, the people of the city bought up every paper they could get their hands on. All three of the city's daily papers had reporters investigating the case, and they published updates about it daily.

Friday's headlines in the *Minneapolis Tribune* and the *Minneapolis Journal* revealed the police determination to talk to the baby's father and to "Widen hunt for father of missing baby."

At the same time, the *Minneapolis Star* claimed that the "Girl mother hopes police find baby taken from hospital."

Alive with police cars and sirens, the city of Minneapolis had become a vibrant metropolis that didn't sleep. The FBI, the Hennepin County attorney, and the State of Minnesota's Bureau of Criminal Apprehension all joined the police in their investigation. Together, they prepared for the return of the alleged father, Larry O'Reilly. A strikingly handsome young man with dark hair and green eyes, O'Reilly had been picked up on August 7th in LaGrange, Illinois. Minneapolis officials wanted him extradited to Minnesota but La-Grange held him, pending a hearing.

Larry's mother used the media to appeal to Margaret and her parents to reveal the location of the baby. Mrs. O'Reilly received no response, but the papers also reported that Margaret's parents said that they would offer a reward for the missing baby, if they had the means to do so.

The evening paper's headline was more troubling to the Bolin family. Eric Sevareid, the cub reporter, was relentless as he investigated every lead and talked to as many people as he could. He covered the story for the *Minneapolis Journal* and, on Saturday, the paper ran his story under the headline, "Mother of Stolen Baby Called to Court!"

Given all of the evidence so far, the Hennepin County Child Welfare League was convinced that Margaret—or her parents—knew the whereabouts of the missing baby girl, so the League obtained a petition ordering Margaret to appear in court with her child and her parents at ten o'clock on Monday morning, August 10th. Under the court order, they had to appear or show just cause as to why they could not.

While the Bolin family was under police surveillance twenty-four hours a day, at least for the time being, the police wanted to put Margaret in jail. The Child Welfare League concurred.

They wanted to guarantee that she would appear in Juvenile Court, where she would be charged as an accessory to baby theft and infanticide.

Thanks to the temporary Chief of Police, however, Margaret remained under guard in her room at General Hospital, because the Chief feared for the young mother's health so soon after delivering a baby. "If they want to get a warrant for the girl, I can't stop them," the Chief told the press. "But they'll have to take her to the Hennepin County Jail, not ours...It's only been eleven days since that missing baby was born, and I'm not going to have that mother's health jeopardized by permitting her removal to jail if I can stop it."

Before Saturday was over, an unlikely player entered the case. Attorney and Minneapolis Alderman Henry H. Bank and his legal associate, James Saks, offered free legal services to Margaret and her family. Bank's involvement in the case surprised many people, to say the least. For one thing, he was Jewish, and anti-Semitism was strong in Minneapolis and elsewhere. Bank had been elected Alderman by the Jewish population who lived in the wealthy wards of North Minneapolis and the nicer suburbs of St. Louis Park—nowhere near the neighborhood where Margaret lived with her impoverished family. He was a powerful man.

Why would Bank volunteer to represent a poor Irish-Catholic girl and her family? Would he really do so for free? Probably not. More likely, someone else was paying him. Not known as an honest attorney, Henry Bank had a reputation as a man who could be bought by anyone who could afford him, including those rumored to be in the mob.

On the other hand, some people who knew Bank were not surprised that the young, flamboyant attorney volunteered to take such a case. A very short man who usually wore a brown suit, Bank nonetheless had a powerful presence that made him seem tall, and he liked to leverage his persona by being in the limelight and making headlines. With a dark, ruddy complexion and piercing black eyes that looked right through people, the man's sense of drama served him well.

Meanwhile, the Hennepin County Child Welfare League continued to explain to Margaret that unwed mothers and their children were normally placed in a nursing home for the first three months of the baby's life. In the Bolin case, the Child Welfare League sought to take custody of Margaret—and her infant, if the young mother knew her whereabouts.

# 7

## COURT

On the morning of Monday, August 10, 1936, well before Margaret's ten o'clock appearance time, the courthouse was crowded with throngs of the curious. People crowded the sidewalk, the steps, and the halls leading to the courtroom. A phalanx of six or seven policewomen and welfare personnel guarded Margaret as she approached the building, protecting her from the angry mob of women who cursed the teenage mother with obscenities, called her names and screaming, "Baby killer!" as she and her guards pressed through the crowd.

Shaken and pale, Margaret finally reached the courtroom, which barred all spectators from the hearing before District Juvenile Judge Winfield William Bardwell. As ordered, Margaret's mother and father attended with her, as well as her aunt, Betsy Bolin, and a cousin, Mrs. Clyde Peterson, but the baby was not in court. Margaret wore a new blue-striped cotton dress, and Margaret's mother wore a matching dress. Bert had purchased both dresses just for the occasion.

Looking like a movie character of a classic judge on the bench, Bardwell presided over the Juvenile Court. With distinguished graying hair, Judge Bardwell was an honest and religious man who freely gave of his time, loved being a judge, and was empathetic toward those who appeared before his court. Nonetheless, as court convened at ten in the morning, the judge noted that both of Margaret's parents had liquor on their breath.

Unusual in juvenile court, the testimony of witnesses was transcribed in this case, the details of which would later be recorded in the newspapers and in county records. As witnesses were called one at a time, the Bolins sat in court, expressionless. The nursery nurses from General Hospital testified to the events prior to the baby's disappearance and then, finally, Margaret was called to testify.

The girl took the stand. Without emotion, she repeated her same story—that a "nurse in blue" had walked out of her room with baby Shirley Ann. That was the only thing that Margaret professed to know, and she insisted upon it without changing her demeanor.

Margaret and her family sat through the hearing, listening to all of the witnesses from General Hospital, and still they shed no tears for Shirley Ann. Indeed, reports claimed that the Bolins seemed relieved that the baby was gone.

County records would reveal that Judge Bardwell could not believe the hard-boiled way that Margaret acted. Once she had recovered from the hecklers on the courthouse steps, the young mother seemed oblivious to the sensationalism of a missing infant and, worse, she seemed cold and uncaring about her own newborn baby. The judge was shocked at her behavior. He acknowledged that most girls Margaret's age were still playing with dolls and going to church with their parents—they were not out all night, drinking, smoking, and making babies—so the judge believed that the teenage mother before him was full of deceit and evil.

When he thought of the missing infant, Shirley Ann, Judge Bardwell strained to keep his composure. As he considered the egregious behavior of the baby's young mother, tears came to his eyes. An honest and decent man, the judge found it difficult to question Margaret without increasing his turmoil.

As the hearing neared its conclusion, the judge declared the missing child a dependent of the Child Welfare League and Margaret a juvenile delinquent. Rather than sending her to jail, he ordered a temporary placement. Margaret was to be placed in a delinquents' home, which the Hennepin County Child Welfare League maintained downtown, on Nicollet Avenue. The "Girls' Club" was like a dormitory, a holding place for delinquent girls whose cases awaited further court and police action against them. For young defendants, it was better than going to jail or to the reformatory, where hardcore criminals presented a danger.

"This baby must be found!" Henry H. Bank announced grandiosely to the press. "I shall make every effort to bring the situation to the grand jury!" Seeking all the headlines that he could get, Bank did not seem to be acting in the interest of his client.

In the evening paper, Eric Sevareid's article was entitled, "Girl mother in court sticks to story," while the Minneapolis Star reiterated the case.

As further confirmation that the case was going nowhere, Margaret's attorney staged a news conference in an attempt to clear the family of suspicion. Henry Bank called for action to restore the baby to her mother, stating that it was entirely possible, as some believed, that the baby was merely being held in someone's home.

"Steps need to be taken," Bank declared, "because that's kidnapping!" Having stated the obvious, Bank called on Mayor Latimore to offer a one thousand dollar reward from the city's contingency fund for information about the whereabouts of the baby, or for the baby to be returned dead or alive. Despite the fact that the fund was low at the time, Bank made the request directly to the Minneapolis City Council, which unanimously voted to offer the reward. In turn, Mayor Latimore declared, "The baby is now worth $1000, dead or alive."

It had been nearly a week since the baby's disappearance, and the police had essentially conducted their investigation without any real clues, other than the cold character and suspicious demeanor of the "girl mother." But, finally, the first solid lead was about to emerge and the police would get the break they needed.

# 8

## THE BLACK BAG

Who knows whether it was because of the publicity or the offer of a reward, but a maid at Minneapolis General Hospital realized that she had seen something early in the morning on the day the baby had vanished. By Tuesday, August 11th, as she followed the story in the papers, the maid realized that the incident may have been significant. She told the hospital superintendent what she had seen and the superintendent immediately called the police.

A small woman who wore glasses, Hilda Hall did laundry, washed floors, and cleaned hospital rooms, starting work at five in the morning. The Wednesday before, soon after she had arrived at work, she had been in the lobby when she noticed two boys walking up the stairs near the hospital's service elevator. Believing that only the death of a relative could have brought the boys to the hospital at such an early hour, Hilda Hall had felt sorry for them, which was why she took particular note of the boys and remembered them.

Fifteen minutes after she noticed them ascending the stairs, she saw the same two boys again, coming down the stairs. This time, one of them was carrying a canvas traveling bag, a cheap, dark satchel with a zipper on the top. The bag was large enough to hold a baby, though it was doubtful that a baby could be alive in the bag.

Hilda Hall also described the boys' appearance. They both appeared to be in their late teens. One wore dark trousers and a white shirt, had dark hair, and looked Jewish. The other was a bushy-haired, plump kid of average height, who wore a dark suit.

Detectives Lehmeyer and Lindholm wondered about the relationship between these boys and the alleged father, Larry O'Reilly, who was still being held in jail in Illinois. The investigators were exploring the validity of the allegation, while the Hennepin assistant attorney contemplated charging O'Reilly with statutory rape. With such charges in mind, the Hennepin prosecutor wanted to question Margaret.

Margaret, on the other hand, had her own plans, which did not include Larry. At seventeen or eighteen years of age, Larry was poor, and so was his family. Margaret did not want to identify a poor man as her baby's father. Instead, she decided to name a very rich Jewish boy. While Margaret considered her options and devised her plan, she refused to swear to the identity of her missing infant's father. As a result, Larry O'Reilly waited, in custody in Illinois.

His mother, however, believed that Larry knew nothing about the baby or the sensational case involving his former girlfriend, Margaret Bolin. As devout Catholics, the O'Reillys were concerned about the missing infant, little Shirley Ann, and they would have offered to take in the baby if they had believed that she belonged to their son. Larry's mother announced to newspaper reporters that she would ask her son about Margaret.

By that evening, however, the newsboys shouted, "Extra! Extra! Read all about it!" Waving the evening *Journal* above their heads, they advertised the headline that ran across the top of the evening paper, shouting, "Baby killed or kidnapped, grand jury to be told." The next day, in an unguarded moment in the County Probation Office, Margaret told Ed Goff, the city's assistant district attorney, that her baby was alive. Just as quickly, she tried to cover up the statement, declaring that she was not positive of the fact. After going over Margaret's declaration, Goff spent an hour interviewing Margaret. In the end, he determined that Margaret gave no indication of being worried over Shirley Ann's whereabouts, while she insisted that she had no knowledge of where her baby had been taken.

The Minneapolis Police Chief announced that he would ask the St. Paul Police Department for the loan of their lie-detector equipment to test the girl mother. (He also requested more assistance from the St. Paul office of the Federal Bureau of Investigation.) Although this announcement was contingent on approval from Margaret's parents, their attorney, Henry Bank, had previously asserted that Margaret would undergo such a test, or any that modern science could devise.

Given Margaret's reluctance to contribute much of substance to the investigation, officials didn't quite know what the truth was or how to find it, so they did all they could to further the case from every angle. While the police followed up on the new clues conveyed by the hospital maid, Hilda Hall, the detectives also kept the pressure on Margaret and her family. Police officers continued to keep Margaret's parents under surveillance, noticing several men in cars parked on the street where the Bolin family lived.

As the couple tried to raise their children and live their lives as they always had, the strain of the case and its sensationalism—on top of the Depression and the heat wave—took its toll on Bert and Barbara, who were almost at their breaking point. And things were only going to get worse for them.

On August 13th, the morning paper declared, "Judge to quiz girl mother about infant." Indeed, the judge had decided to question Margaret in his chambers to see if he could appeal to her to tell the truth. He sent a squad car to retrieve Margaret from the Nicollet Avenue Girls' Club and bring her to his chambers.

Judge Bardwell waited until Margaret arrived, wearing her cotton striped dress under her bob-style haircut. She was allowed to wear make-up, which she did, with red lipstick. She smiled at the judge.

"Have a seat," the judge said in a paternalistic tone. "Now, let's get down to business, young lady." He stood over the girl and looked at her, while she sat silently, looking scared to death. "Tell me what really happened to your baby," he demanded with a lively glint in his eyes as he waited for her to answer his question. She sat there, stiff, while the judge was deep in thought. Finally, he raised his eyebrows and bellowed, "I'm giving you a chance to talk!"

Judge Bardwell's gavel accidentally fell to the floor, causing Margaret to panic. She jumped to her feet. "It was the nurse in blue," she blurted. "She took my baby!"

The judge's face remained somber as he stared at her. "Doesn't it scare you that your baby might have been murdered?"

Margaret flinched, blinking her eyes. "I know my baby's alive," she burst out. Then her voice softened as she considered his question. "Who would kill her?" she asked, as if the idea of murder had never occurred to her.

"That's what I'm asking you," Judge Bardwell said after a long pause.

Margaret looked desperate. Finally, she cried crocodile tears. "I don't know!"

The judge's face grew hard. "I don't believe that you really care about what happened to your baby daughter."

Though the judge may have been right, Margaret seemed more concerned about what might happen to her, not to her baby. "I'm innocent," she pleaded in response to his accusation. "It was the nurse in blue. She did it."

"It's a horrible thing to live with a secret of this magnitude," the compassionate judge said sympathetically, staring at her, trying to break her. Softly, he added, "Now, come on and tell me the truth, once and for all."

"I feel sick," Margaret said as sweat trickled down her neck, soaking the collar of her cotton dress. "It's too hot. I swear, I'm going to be sick. I'm going to throw up!"

Judge Bardwell decided that it was hopeless. He wondered whether the hard times of the Great Depression had driven Margaret, at her young age, to prostitution. But, still, he wondered, why had she become the way she was? How could she not care about her own baby?

In the end, Judge Bardwell realized that it didn't much matter, and he didn't really care. The girl was obviously beyond help and the judge was much more concerned about baby Shirley Ann, a poor abandoned baby, who had possibly been murdered. As he thought of the precious baby dead, tears came to Judge Bardwell's eyes.

The county attorney also continued to pursue the case. He indicated that he was not satisfied that Larry O'Reilly was actually the father of the missing baby, as he believed that Margaret was covering up facts in order to protect someone. The authorities were at a loss, however. They did not know what to do with the girl, who was obviously keeping important information from the officials. It was clear that Margaret Bolin was a liar, but the police couldn't search every home in Minneapolis, or drag every Minneapolis lake, in search of the missing baby.

As the case limped along, Margaret had no credibility with anyone, not the judge, the county attorney, or the police detectives. Aware of the girl's long history of lying to her parents and everyone else, they questioned her veracity, while the press and the community vilified Margaret. Decent people who followed the case felt shocked and dismayed that the young mother and her family seemed to care so little about the missing baby and, to everyone working on the case, it had become as repulsive as it was frustrating. But by the end of the week, the investigation was in full gear and the detectives could barely keep up.

With his flair for the dramatic, Henry Bank contended that the baby had been kidnapped and, since the alleged father was in another state, the baby probably was, too. Playing with the press and the authorities, Bank announced that he was pleading with the Bureau of Investigation and Department of Justice to put their crack G-men on the case. It was just an act. Bank kept his information close to the vest, and knew much more than he let on—most of it well before he volunteered to represent Margaret and the Bolins. After all, somebody was paying him, and it was not Margaret's penniless family.

As for Bank's request for federal help in the case, he hardly needed to request it. The Federal Bureau of Investigation had already opened a file on the kidnapped baby and, in the wake of the Lindbergh kidnapping, even J. Edgar Hoover was closely watching the Minneapolis investigation. The Lindbergh case had put Hoover's FBI on the map, granted the agency incredible powers, and moved Congress to pass the Lindbergh Law, making kidnapping a federal crime that was punishable by death, so federal investigators were following the local officials' progress—or lack of it.

Henry Bank had also floated a flamboyant request in the media, requesting that investigators give Margaret a lie detector test. But, by Friday, August 14, assistant district attorney Ed Goff refused, saying that he would never subject a fifteen-year-old girl to such a test. It didn't matter. Before anything else happened, a bulletin came over the police wires, changing everything. About ninety miles north of Minneapolis, two teenage boys had found the drowned body of an infant girl, stuffed into a black canvas satchel, just outside of the village of Willow River.

# 9

# The Willow River Baby

The western point of Lake Superior is shaped like the tip of an index finger that points from a fist down toward the village of Willow River, about fifty miles southwest of the world's largest lake. In those parts of Pine County, Minnesota, the sheriff was Hannes Rypkema, a pure law-and-order man who was charged with investigating the drowning death of a beautiful baby girl, who looked to be two or three weeks old. Removing her body from the cheap canvas bag, the sheriff pulled out a soggy stack of *True Story and True Romance* magazines that had been laid in the bottom of the bag, presumably to weigh it down in the cold Willow River. It didn't work. But the top of the bag had been left unzipped so that water would rush in and fill the bag, drowning the baby. Sadly, that did work.

"The baby had only been in the Willow River two hours or less," Sheriff Rypkema explained to reporters. "So its body was in good shape, despite the overwhelming heat." The news hit the wire services and, in no time, newsrooms all across the country knew that a young baby had been found, dead.

Rypkema and his colleagues were no doubt aware of the sensational case ninety miles to the south, that of a newborn girl who had recently been kidnapped from a Minneapolis hospital. With that in mind, law enforcement officials in Pine County, Minnesota, generated an all-points bulletin so that all police departments would hear the news, which also reached the newspapers, informing them that the body of a baby girl had been found, drowned, a quarter of a mile north of Willow River Village in Pine County.

Officials took the body eight miles south to Finlayson, where they used the funeral parlor as a morgue. They laid the baby out on an orange crate and covered her with a pillow case. Curious children tried to sneak peeks at the body as it turned blue.

Baking in the oppressive heat of the August afternoon, officials at the Minneapolis Police Department got word that the body of a female infant had been found up north. Despite the heat and humidity, every corner of the Police Department bounced into high gear.

Detectives John Lehmeyer and Harry Lindholm quickly realized that the Willow River baby was the same age as their kidnapped infant, Shirley Ann Bolin, who had been missing for nine days. The detectives instantly connected the news to their case and, as all the pieces seemed to fit, they assumed that the dead infant was baby Shirley Ann. Lehmeyer blinked a few times as he processed the information.

Other than the hospital nurses, few people cared as much as Lehmeyer and Lindholm about what had become of baby Shirley

Ann. They were certain that they cared more than the baby's young mother, and they were much more invested—both personally and professionally—than the public, despite the desperation with which the public wanted to know every detail of the case.

To identify the Willow River baby, Lehmeyer and Lindholm arranged to take a couple of their witnesses to Finlayson. Since several nurses at Minneapolis General Hospital had cared for Shirley Ann, the investigators needed to see if the nurses could identify the drowned baby as the missing one. They thought it would be simple—and their reprehensible case would finally be solved. It was sad, but at least it would be over.

The detectives drove to the hospital and picked up two nurses, and then they drove the seventy-five miles north to the funeral parlor in Finlayson.

The detectives asked the nurses to go in, one at a time, to view the body of the Willow River baby. Each nurse entered the room and conducted an extensive examination, looking at the baby's face, scalp, and body. Both of the nurses rolled the baby over, looking at her back. Emerging from the room, the nurses gave similar reports. Though they agreed that both the Willow River baby and Shirley Ann Bolin were beautiful, and both were two to three weeks old, those were the only similarities. Shirley Ann had a lot of curly hair, but the deceased Willow River baby did not. Also, the Willow River baby bore marks of forceps on her head, while Shirley Ann Bolin had no such marks.

Further, in Minneapolis General Hospital, the nurses stuck an adhesive square to the back of every newborn—between the shoulder blades—writing the mother's name, the baby's sex, and the date of birth on the sticker. These squares used very strong adhesive, the nurses explained, and they were terrible to remove from the tender skin of newborns. Doing so damaged the young skin, leaving telltale marks. But the Willow River baby had no such tape on her back, nor any sign of such tape having been removed. Both of the nurses were certain: The Willow River baby in the makeshift morgue was not the missing Shirley Ann Bolin from Minneapolis General Hospital.

Detectives Lehmeyer and Lindholm did not know what to make of it.

Later in the day, the Minneapolis Police Department sent two more hospital nurses up to Finlayson to identify the dead infant. One of those nurses agreed with the first two, saying that she was certain that the dead baby was not the infant from Minneapolis General Hospital.

The other nurse couldn't make up her mind. Finally, the detectives and nurses returned to Minneapolis.

Once the funeral parlor was quiet, Pine County's deputy coroner examined the baby. Eventually, the official record would state that the baby had been "thrown into the river with criminal intent."

Back in Minneapolis, the police told Margaret Bolin about the Willow River baby. Though the nurses had sworn that the dead baby was not Shirley Ann, the police told Margaret that they believed the dead baby to be hers. As the interrogations intensified, Margaret sobbed, terrified that she would be charged with murder. Indeed, the district attorney ordered Margaret jailed.

After a three-hour grilling, Margaret finally broke her silence and offered a few juicy morsels to stimulate the investigation, steering it away from herself. She insisted that her baby was alive and well, ands he admitted that Larry O'Reilly, whom she had originally accused, was not the baby's father. Rather, she said, a seventeen-year-old boy named Mike Osman was the father of the missing baby Shirley Ann. Margaret also happened to add that a blonde seamstress who was friends with Mike Osman had taken the baby.

The police wasted no time. Immediately, they located Mike, picked him up, and brought him to the city jail. A soft-spoken Jewish boy, Mike had a dark face surrounded by black hair, which he wore slicked back. His real name was Mitchell Osman. He had perfect manners, wore natty clothes, and he was extremely affluent. Mike's widowed mother had remarried and, when she did, she married money—lots of money. One of the wealthiest families in the city, Mike's family owned significant property, including liquor stores and taverns, in downtown Minneapolis and elsewhere.

Under further questioning, Margaret continued to insist that Mike was the father and she shared what she knew about him. Margaret revealed that Mike was employed at his family's cigar store on Marquette Avenue.

From there, police were able to identify and question another girlfriend of Mike's, who provided names of a couple of his friends, George and Vernon. The detectives were eager to locate Mike's friend who had a lighter complexion and bushy hair.

The police also found out that the seamstress, named Agnes Hermanson, was a twenty-four-year-old woman from North Minneapolis. Locating the woman, the police immediately searched her room, particularly looking for articles of dress, such as a blue uniform. Though the detectives did not find any pertinent evidence, they held the seamstress as the suspected abductor.

Working the case for the *Minneapolis Journal*, Eric Sevareid had four stories in the paper that evening, two stories about the Minneapolis angle and two stories about the new aspect of the case, the Willow River developments.

Before long, Margaret's fellow inmates at the delinquents' home claimed that Margaret had told them that, two months before her baby was born, she and Mike had planned to have the baby taken care of. When the police questioned Margaret about these witnesses' claims, she flatly denied having said any such thing. The police subjected her to further intense questioning, this time asking her why she had named Larry O'Reilly as the father. Margaret explained that she "liked him best."

Police also learned that another nurse had liked baby Shirley Ann so much that she had taken a picture of the infant. The nurse had gone to Montana on vacation, leaving the film to be developed in Chicago, and she was presumably unaware of the disappearance and ensuing investigation. The police followed up on the lead and attempted to obtain the photograph and talk to the nurse.

At nine o'clock in the morning on August 15th, Detectives Lehmeyer and Lindholm conducted a line-up at the hospital. First, they wanted to see if the hospital maid, Hilda Hall, could identify Mike as one of the young men she had seen on the morning of the baby's disappearance. Mike, who had a dark complexion, was one of five men in the line-up. Hilda Hall was sure that Mike was one of the men she had seen with a black zippered traveling bag, walking up the hospital stairs soon after she arrived at work, early on the morning of August 5th.

Encouraged by the positive identification, the police asked a few other General Hospital employees, including an orderly, to have a look at the line-up. The orderly had reported that he had seen two young men at about nine in the evening on August 4th, the night before the baby went missing. According to his description, the men were seventeen to nineteen years of age. One had a dark complexion while the other had light, bushy hair. The orderly was certain that Mike was the dark-haired man of the pair that he had seen that night.

The hospital's switchboard operator, who had been on duty on August 4th, also told the police that she had seen two young men in the lobby of General Hospital. According to the operator, the men hung around for an hour and a half before they finally went upstairs. Like the orderly, the telephone operator described the young men as seventeen to nineteen years of age, and one of them was dark while the other had light, bushy hair. The operator had further explained that the bushy-haired boy had drawn her attention because he had stumbled on a step while going up the stairs. Later, when she went off duty and left the building, she noticed the same two boys standing outside the hospital, talking. At the line-up, she identified Mike as the dark-haired man.

The switchboard operator, however, refused to sign a statement testifying to the fact that the man in the line-up was the man at the hospital. Afraid of making a mistake, she did not want to positively identify anyone, particularly someone who might have been wealthy and well-connected. At the conclusion of the line-up, the switchboard operator expressed her fear.

It was common for witnesses to fear their role in implicating someone in a crime, especially if that someone was rich. Families like Mike Osman's, who had money, also had power, and they controlled banks, jobs, everything in the city. Any witnesses who might have had information that was antagonistic to Mike may well have felt afraid or threatened with being run out of town or losing their jobs, which was a tremendous threat during the Great Depression. In a corrupt city like Minneapolis—and in an age of lost innocence for poor people— common folks feared the rich and powerful, who often had ties to the Minnesota Mafia.

The Minnesota Mafia, which consisted primarily of rich and aggressive Jewish businessmen, was one of the largest and better-organized groups in Minneapolis during the 1930s. In the city, it had all the power—more than the police departments, prosecutors, mayors, or anyone else. Through the Minnesota Mafia, the rich controlled the city and trampled on its less privileged citizens.

Regardless, Minneapolis police were certain that Margaret's boyfriend, Mike Osman, was the missing link to baby Shirley Ann. They were determined to find out all they could about the young Jewish man and his acquaintances.

Police were able to locate Mike's friends, Vernon Hanson and George Haggberg. George, who had heaps of bushy, light-colored hair, was married and worked at a filling station. The police brought him in and got a statement from him, then took him to the lobby of Minneapolis General Hospital to see if witnesses could identify him. Though the hospital employees said that George resembled the bushy-haired youth who had been with Mike the night before the abduction, the witnesses were reluctant to positively identify the young man. The police released him, though they instructed him to report to police headquarters the following morning.

As Lehmeyer and Lindholm followed the leads, talking to Mike's friends and relatives, they heard that Mike had been out of town at the time of the baby's disappearance, having taken a ten-day trip to relieve his hay fever. According to the witnesses, Mike had gone north, to Duluth, Minnesota, and Superior, Wisconsin, returning home at about five o'clock in the morning on August 6th, almost exactly twenty-four hours after the baby disappeared. But Eric Sevareid, reporting for the *Minneapolis Journal*, checked the hotels in Duluth, where Mike had supposedly stayed, and he could find no registration records showing that Mike Osman had been in Duluth.

Mike then said that he had stayed at a hotel in Superior, Wisconsin, and that he had checked out of the hotel on August 2nd, but also that he had driven his car home from Superior at five in the morning on August 5th. In another breath, he claimed that he had left Superior at about six in the morning. Later, Mike admitted to returning to Minneapolis after leaving the hotel in Superior, Wisconsin, but, apparently, he had been there only in late July, from the 27th through the 29th, not into August and certainly not as late as August 5th.

The Minneapolis police later received a letter from the Duluth police department, stating that they had taken possession of a letter, dated August 1st, addressed to Mike Osman at the Spaulding Hotel. The letter, from a girlfriend of Mike's, had been at a Duluth Hotel, unclaimed, for some time. Though the letter seemed to prove that Mike was not in Duluth in August, the Minneapolis police inspected the letter and determined that it contained nothing of importance, so they turned it over to Mike, who sat in the city jail.

Police then learned that after Mike had left the hotel in Superior, Wisconsin, he had returned to Minneapolis on July 29th, registering at a Minneapolis hotel under the alias Michael Swiller. Mike claimed to have stayed at the Minneapolis hotel for a week, though a clerk revealed that he had been at the hotel for only one night.

With all of Mike Osman's contradictory claims and suspicious movements, including being in Duluth—just forty-seven miles from the village of Willow River—it would have been reasonable for police to investigate any connection he might have had to the dead Willow River baby. But there is no record that the police in Minneapolis or in Pine County investigated this relationship. Why?

Mike Osman's family was rich. They could afford hush money, they could afford to hire Henry Bank (who would keep Margaret under wraps), and they could afford to buy Mike protection from the law. That was the nature of Minneapolis in the 1930s.

Police did, however, hold Mike in jail for a time, grilling him about his relationship with Margaret and his whereabouts at the time of the baby's disappearance. Mike continued to insist that he had met Margaret at a dance and that he had never been intimate with her. As a result of his insistence—and for other reasons, as well—the police sought to get a written statement of paternity from Margaret.

The county attorney said that, if he could obtain this statement, he could turn the case over to the grand jury. While the county attorney conducted his own investigation of the case, for some reason he had turned lukewarm on an immediate grand jury investigation and, in the end, the grand jury never got the case. Again, it was likely that Mike's wealthy family pulled some strings, with the help of Margaret's attorney, Henry Bank.

Still, Mike's unexplained movements and contradictions regarding his whereabouts obviously made him look guilty and, if law enforcement wasn't going to pursue him, the media would. On August

15th, Eric Sevareid wrote this about Mike in the *Minneapolis Journal*:

*He didn't care at all about the missing baby, possibly his own daughter. He only cared about himself. He was rich and cocky, a very wild kid and lied all the time and always nattily dressed. He only wanted girlfriends for his own pleasure, buying beer to get the girls drunk. That's what he considered a good time. Of course his money bought him all of those things. His bedroom eyes were always on the lookout for his next girlfriend and a hotel to spend the night.*

Eric Sevareid also researched the black travel bag in which the Willow River baby had been drowned. Sevareid was able to discover the origin of the bag, which had some clear marks on the bottom, according to Sheriff Rypkema.

On the first or second of August, a woman named Marlys Johnson had been at her job, working as a clerk at a drugstore at 8th and Marquette Avenue in downtown Minneapolis. The clerk noticed a nervous-looking young man, who came into the store with a friend. "Good afternoon," Marlys said, looking up at the man's bushy heap of light-colored hair. "May I help you?"

"Yeah," said the man, who looked to be about twenty years old. "I need a bag to carry baby things," he said, adding that he wanted a bag that was eighteen to twenty inches long. Since he was particular about the size, Marlys found a canvas traveling bag of the right dimensions. It was a cheap black bag with a zipper on the top.

As she sold him the bag, she noticed that the varnish from the drugstore shelves had transferred to the bottom of the bag and it had varnish marks on it. She looked at the customer and his friend, who was dressed sharply and wore his black hair slicked back. The young men did not seem to notice or care about the varnish marks. After the blonde man purchased the bag, the two of them walked out the door to into the August heat of downtown Minneapolis.

Detectives Lindholm and Lehmeyer followed up on the lead, eager to further prove the connection between Mike and the canvas bag in which the Willow River baby was found. Indeed, the drugstore clerk was able to clinch her identification of the bag by the varnish marks on it.

Since Mike was known to have had many girlfriends in northern Minnesota, the detectives' theory was that he had used the bag to sneak Margaret's baby out of the hospital, and then used it again to drown baby Shirley Ann—or another infant—ninety miles north, in the Willow River.

With so many leads, the investigators were just trying to follow up with all the clues in the case. At least there was finally a break in the weather. On August 16th, though the mercury hit 102.8 degrees, it rained in Minneapolis, breaking the dank humidity and the sixty-day drought.

That day, Margaret suddenly had a new revelation for the detectives. She accused Mike Osman of sneaking into her room and stealing her baby. Since Margaret had already changed her story a few times, the detectives did not know what to believe. For the third time, they interrogated Mike, but they learned nothing of significance.

The next day, August 17th, was even busier, as Detectives Lehmeyer and Lindholm continued to follow the clues wherever they led. Interested to learn whether medical professionals could analyze blood from Margaret and from the dead baby found at Willow River, they called on a medical doctor, Doctor Seashore in Minneapolis. They wanted to know whether it was possible to determine if the two persons had the same blood type and if they were related. Dr. Seashore said that he could not perform such a test but that Dr. Bell at the University might have that capability. However, such a test would require legal action and would involve considerable expense. As much as the detectives wanted to know whether the Willow River baby was Shirley Ann, even municipalities and their law enforcement departments were constrained by the Great Depression. They decided not to attempt the blood test.

Though the seamstress, Agnes Hermanson, was in custody, she heard about the discovery of the dead baby in Willow River. She also heard that Margaret was repeatedly telling authorities that "Agnes the seamstress" was the one who came into her hospital room that morning and carried away the baby. "It's a lie," the young woman declared. "It's a lie!"

Agnes wanted to speak to Margaret, to confront her face-to-face. The police arranged the meeting and took Agnes to meet the young mother. "You say that I did this to you," Agnes said when she met Margaret. "Why? I don't even know you. I didn't even know your name, because I've never had anything to do with you! Why would you say that I did this?" Margaret stamped her feet. "You're the one that took my baby!" she insisted.

Agnes, however, told the police that, when the baby had been taken, she had been in her home to Alexandria, Minnesota, about 130 miles away. Police checked out the woman's story and determined that she had an iron-clad alibi.

The pressure started coming from all directions. In addition to the Minneapolis detectives, authorities in Pine County pushed their own investigation to determine the identity of the Willow River baby. Unfortunately—and for unknown reasons—they did not question Mike about that aspect of the case, despite the fact that Minneapolis investigators suspected him of buying the black bag that was used to drown the infant.

On another front, the policewoman who was in charge of the Women's Bureau where Margaret was detained announced that Margaret had told her that sometime before the baby's birth on July 27th, Mike had threatened to kill Margaret and her baby after the birth. As a result, the county attorney decided to have another session with Margaret on August 17th. But, first, the county attorney told the press that investigators were making arrangements for Margaret to view the body of the dead Willow River baby, to see if she could identify it.

With her attorney, Henry Bank, Margaret left Minneapolis with a large entourage of police, attorneys, and reporters, who all headed north to the makeshift morgue in the Finlayson funeral home. With the relentless and extreme heat, the ninety-mile drive to the funeral home was long and miserable.

When they arrived, Margaret was silently led into the parlor, where the afternoon heat was punctuated by the white glare of a dangling light bulb. Though the police had been unable to penetrate Margaret's tough skin for twelve days, the detectives believed reality would finally break her.

The body of the dead baby was placed in front of her. Without speaking, Margaret looked at the infant. After a moment, she gazed into the baby girl's eyes, which were the color of her own. The young mother touched the baby's hair, which felt just like her own hair, and then she ran her fingertips over the baby's nose, her cheekbones, and her mouth.

Margaret turned away. "Maybe," she whispered. "My baby's hair was darker."

"Well," said the coroner solemnly, "the hair on the back of the head is considerably darker."

Margaret nodded as she looked again at the baby. Her mouth began to quiver and then she burst into soft, restrained sobs. "That's my baby," she cried as tears streamed down her cheeks. "It's my baby!"

Henry Bank touched her arm and drew her aside. "Are you sure?" he asked in a whisper. "You must be sure."

"It's mine," she insisted, nodding.

After another moment of silence, the doctor pulled up the pillowcase, covering the face of the murdered baby. "I've never seen a more beautiful baby," he said.

Margaret began to cry convulsively. "I didn't know it was going to be killed," she said. "My family didn't know anything about it at all." Regaining her composure, Margaret pointed out that the baby was not wearing the same clothing that she had worn the last time she had seen her, but the young mother again said that she was positive that the infant was her child, baby Shirley Ann.

Since Margaret was considerably shaken, a policewoman led her outside and then a county investigator took her a few doors down to a confectionery and bought Margaret a bottle of Coke. As she drank the soda, Margaret swooned, breaking into a paroxysm of weeping. It was some time before she regained her composure.

Finally, Margaret started talking. She said that her family didn't even know Mike but that he did not want to support Margaret or her baby, even if the newborn was his. Margaret further explained that, when Mike had visited her at General Hospital on August 4th, they had planned the baby's disappearance. Margaret claimed that she had given the baby to Mike in the hospital, while he was staying at a hotel in the downtown Minneapolis loop. Originally, she said, Mike was going to give the baby to some friends, a married couple, but then he decided to drown it in Lake Calhoun in Minneapolis. She also said that, before the baby was born, she had seen a black canvas bag in the rear seat of Mike's car.

According to Margaret, she and Mike had met in 1935 at the South Side Tavern, where Mike's brother, Al, tended bar. A year later, nearly full-term in her pregnancy, Margaret was still a naïve girl. She did not understand that men from wealthy families do not marry poor girls, but soon enough she realized that Mike would not marry her, whether she was pregnant with his baby or not. Still, she hoped that having his baby—or what he thought was his baby—would help her get her hands on some of the Osman family's money. But Mike Osman was a dangerous playmate for Margaret, who would have been a young fourteen years old when she conceived Shirley Ann. Today, such a man would be arrested as a child molester, a sexual predator. But, in 1936, "promiscuous" young girls—especially impoverished ones—were seen as playthings. Men and society did not respect loose woman, but it was perfectly acceptable for men to have a woman—or women—on the side. Mike wanted sex from a beautiful girl and he got it, for the price of a few beers. Margaret was just another pawn in Mike's ample stable of girls from everywhere in Minnesota. Though she had hoped that such a boy would lavish her with Myrna Loy's

*Thin Man* lifestyle, Margaret would get little in return for her sexual favors or her pregnancy.

Margaret paid a high price for her naiveté and, other than pain, the only thing she actually obtained from her relationship with Mike was a very expensive attorney, Henry H. Bank.

Given Margaret's story, the police concluded that Margaret and Mike had plotted to dispose of the baby by killing it. The police further concluded that the original plan had not taken into consideration that the baby would be born at Minneapolis General Hospital. The premature birth likely necessitated a plan B: a hastily-planned abduction from the hospital.

Eric Sevareid's article in the *Minneapolis Journal* publicized the progress in the case on one of the biggest days in the investigation to date. "Goff Uncovers Hot Tip from Mother of Missing Baby" was the evening headline on August 17th. And though Margaret's revelations were the headline, officials had made other significant progress that day.

Looking into Mike's involvement, Lehmeyer and Lindholm took the young man to the drugstore located downtown, near the cigar store where Mike worked, to see if the clerks could identify him. Unfortunately, Marlys Johnson and her coworker could not be sure whether Mike had accompanied the buyer of the bag, but they remembered well the youth with bushy blond hair as the purchaser. If only they could get a look at the other young man—Mike's buddy with the bushy hair.

The officials arranged to have George brought to the office of the county attorney, and then they called in Marlys Johnson. As they paraded George before the clerk, she identified him as the bushy-haired young man who had purchased the canvas bag. She was certain of it.

"Girl Mother Declares Dead Baby Hers," declared the Friday morning headline in the *Minneapolis Tribune*. When he heard the news, Mike began pacing back and forth inside his Minneapolis jail cell. "Golly!" he cried. "She's really scared me now, but I didn't have a thing to do with it!" Deep worry lines bit into his forehead as tears popped up into his eyes. "It's a lie!" he claimed, suggesting that Margaret was likely lying to protect someone else. "I had nothing to do with it! It's a lie!" Mike continued. Finally he did admit to having taken Margaret out on several occasions, but he repeated his denial of having had an illicit relationship with the girl.

Mike's mother, Jenny Osman, who had sworn to her son's innocence, visited him that day. Learning of Margaret's statement that the dead baby was hers, Mrs. Osman began to cry before she left the jail. "My son had nothing to do with it," she said to reporters on the courthouse steps. "He told me that he was innocent, and he was telling the truth. Ever since he was a child, I could always get the truth from him. He has been a good boy. I always told him to come home early every night, and he said that he must have some recreation, but he is good and he is innocent. Please don't persecute my boy," she pleaded, fearing that her son would be vilified because he was Jewish. "I am certain he is telling the truth this time."

Later that day, while Mike's cell was being cleaned, he was put in the Women's Bureau of the jail, where he ran into the seamstress, Agnes. She had been one of Mike's drinking friends and they were acquainted with one another. Agnes had just heard about Margaret's identification of the dead baby and, like Mike, she was upset.

"Come on, kid," Mike said to her. "Buck up! Can't you take it? We're both under the rap," he added. "Margaret put it on both of us."

Finally, Detectives Lehmeyer and Lindholm decided to conduct a joint questioning, examining Margaret and Mike together in order to study their reactions. By the time the police brought the two together, Margaret was composed as she insisted that Mike was the father of her baby. For his part, Mike continued to deny ever being intimate with the fifteen-year-old girl. To contradict him, Margaret named hotels where they had stayed, including the Stockholm Hotel in downtown Minneapolis. She even described the interiors of the rooms they had occupied at the Stockholm and elsewhere.

The next day, the police checked out the lead. They went to 300 South 3rd Street and entered the Stockholm Hotel, where they questioned a night clerk. They learned that Mike had spent a good deal of money at the hotel, drinking with Margaret and their friends. Mike bought many five-cent glasses of beer to get his pals and Margaret drunk. The clerk further revealed that Mike and his friends, Earl and Ed, took three girls to rooms in the hotel, and Margaret was one of the girls. To rent the rooms, Mike left his watch as security. The next day, Mike returned, paid for the rooms, and retrieved his watch.

The detectives related the clerk's recollections to Mike, whose tough-guy persona disintegrated. "Okay! I slept with her," he admitted, starting to weep. "We had sex all night, but there's no way I'm the father of that baby!"

"Why's that?" Lindholm asked.

"I always used rubbers!" the young man asserted.

The detectives shook their heads. "They're not too reliable, Mike," said Lehmeyer. Mike continued to cry. At seventeen years of age, his lies and crimes—including statutory rape, at least—had caught up with him. At least, he thought they had.

On the morning of August 20th, the paper announced, "Youth in Baby Case to Face Court Today on Statutory Charge." By that evening, Eric Sevareid reported under the headline, "Charge Filed Against Youth in Baby Case." The Hennepin County Judge had ordered the county attorney to release Mike from custody if he did not take action by filing charges against him by ten a.m. The charge of statutory rape would put the case into juvenile court, giving authorities additional time to round out their investigation, so the county attorney responded to the judge's order by filing the formal charge of statutory rape against Mike.

In many ways, August 20th was a day for legal wrangling. The attorney for Agnes prepared to file a writ of habeas corpus, as the seamstress had been held without charges for five days. Also, the Sheriff of Pine County and the State Crime Bureau agents came to Minneapolis to confer with Hennepin County officials regarding the identification of the Willow River baby.

Finally, Minneapolis authorities announced that, if murder charges were to be filed later, they should not be served in Minneapolis but in Pine County, where the baby's body had been found. However, if the Willow River baby had been kidnapped from Minneapolis General Hospital prior to the murder, then Minneapolis would have been the proper jurisdiction and the city—not Pine County—should file charges against Mike Osman and Margaret Bolin.

Indeed, Pine County's Sheriff Hannes Rypkema felt that something was wrong in Minneapolis, that something was being hushed up regarding Mike and his culpability. The Pine County officials even wondered if Mike had fathered two babies, both born at about the same time. For their part, Minneapolis officials would not comment on the reliability of Margaret's claim that the Willow River baby was hers. But some witnesses did.

In General Hospital, the nurses who had viewed the deceased baby in the Finlayson funeral parlor made a pronouncement through a spokesperson, the nursery supervisor. "Nine thousand babies we have seen come and go out of General Hospital," said the supervisor. "Some may say babies change a lot and they change rapidly, but I don't see how we could have been mistaken." The spokesperson added. "It's part of our business to know and recognize these babies, and we often become attached to them. This was such a pretty one, everybody liked her. It doesn't seem logical that the baby could change so rapidly." The nurses' statement made it clear: The Willow River baby was a different child.

But given Margaret's statement, as the mother, that the dead baby was hers, the crucial question remained: Was baby Shirley Ann the Willow River baby? Or were there two babies, one dead and one still missing?

In order to prosecute the case, officials would have to prove that the dead baby was baby Shirley Ann, missing from General Hospital. But how could a prosecutor prove this, when the police's own witnesses—three nurses from General Hospital's nursery—had already asserted that it was not the same baby? They could have had the blood analyzed at the University but, given the economic constraints of the Great Depression, the city refused to spend the money on the test, though it would have proved once and for all whether the babies were one and the same. The only other party to the case, who certainly could have paid for the blood test, was Mike's family, but they never offered to contribute this assistance to the resolution of the case, perhaps for obvious reasons.

Since Mike remained detained by the police, the young man's attorney requested that the juvenile judge free Mike unless prosecutors filed charges or set bond if they did file charges.

In a bit of legal maneuvering early in the day, the county attorney's office had a female police attendant from the Women's Bureau swear a formal complaint, and then the county attorney's office notified the district juvenile judge that the State had no objection to the issuance of the writ.

As detectives ushered Mike into court, he was smartly dressed in a brown suit with his dark hair slicked back as usual. According to reporters, the young defendant had a smirk on his face.

Hennepin County officials acknowledged that the evidence against Mike was purely circumstantial, but they felt it was sufficient to justify holding him. They persisted in wanting Mike detained so that they could continue to grill him about his role in the baby's disappearance.

Though the judge granted the writ, Hughes acknowledged that he anticipated that Mike would be rearrested upon leaving the courtroom. Further, the attorney advised his client to remain in the courtroom while he attempted to arrange bail, which was set at one thousand dollars. A detective guarded Mike, who remained for some time before he was rearrested. With the smirk gone from his face, Mike was taken back to jail.

Later that day, Minneapolis police began investigating a new lead. According to a tip, two friends of Mike's had taken a sudden trip eastward, to Wisconsin. Though Mike never admitted to taking this trip, these two friends had apparently visited Mike while he was staying at the Stockholm Hotel in downtown Minneapolis from August 1st until the 6th, the day after the baby disappeared. The information about the hotel corroborated Margaret's claim that Mike was staying there when the baby went missing.

To police, it seemed as if the girl mother might have been telling the truth, for once. Still, the case had many loose ends, and it was about to get a few more.

# 10

## Muddle

Pine County's sheriff Hannes Rypkema turned over all of his evidence in the case of the Willow River baby on August 21st.

He provided the file to the Minnesota Bureau of Criminal Apprehension in St. Paul and then no one ever saw it again. However, the sheriff also gave his records to Detectives Lehmeyer and Lindholm of the Minneapolis Police Department. When he handed over the file, the sheriff also told detectives about an unusual scene that had taken place on August 12th, the day before the Willow River baby was found.

It was well after midnight the night before when a 1932 or 1933 black Chevrolet Coach emerged from thick fog and pulled into a service station a mile north of Willow River. The driver was a young woman in her early twenties and her car had a flat tire. Driving conditions were extremely hazardous, which made the owners of the service station wonder what could possibly bring a young woman out alone on such a night.

She weighed about one-hundred-twenty pounds and her slender body was wrapped in a three-quarters-length light tan overcoat, which she wore with white shoes trimmed in brown. She had a light complexion and light hair that was cut in a bob and held back with a half-inch ribbon that was tied in a bow on top. Finishing her outfit, she carried a large black purse with a zippered cigarette case.

The owner of the Skelly Oil Station, Randall Stanton, went about changing the tire on the woman's car. He was not the only one who heard faint noises coming from inside the Chevy.

While Randall changed the tire, a couple of brothers, Leo and Ted Price, took the woman for a walk. The three of them walked about a mile together.

"How deep is the river?" she asked. "Oh, six or eight feet," they told her.

"My," she said, changing the subject. "Do you know how far it is to Duluth?"

"About fifty miles," they answered.

"Do you think ten gallons of gas will be enough to get me through?" They figured it would.

After Randall Stanton put on the spare tire, the woman bought the gas and left.

The men decided that they had heard the gentle whimpering of a newborn baby in the back seat of the woman's car.

The detectives followed up on the information. The only possible link they could think of was that the woman might have been the wife of Mike's friend, George, but the description did not add up.

That evening, Eric Sevareid's article in the *Minneapolis Journal* reflected the frustration of investigators in the case: "Baby Muddle is

Left Where Inquiry Began," declared the headline. And Margaret was about to add to the muddle yet again. As the detectives resumed questioning Margaret on August 22nd, she told them that a middle-aged fireman from South Minneapolis was the kidnapper of her baby!

Flabbergasted, the police investigators took Margaret to the grand jury room to get her formal statement. Margaret said that she'd had intimate relations with the man, Edward T. Howie, who had taken her on automobile rides in his 1936 convertible. He had also taken her out to theaters and had given her money, clothes, and jewelry. In return, Margaret apparently rendered her usual services. Though Margaret insisted that Mike Osman, with all his money, was the baby's father, she also declared that the fireman had given her money, offered to provide for the baby's expenses, and it was he who had spirited away the baby on August 5th.

Pursuing the lead, the detectives learned that Edward Howie was a forty-four-year-old fire captain, one of the most popular men on the squadron, and the father of four children. Lehmeyer and Lindholm picked him up, held him in the Minneapolis jail, and then took him to the county attorney's office to get his formal statement. While the fireman admitted to befriending Margaret, he insisted that he'd had nothing more than a fatherly interest in her. Meanwhile, his buddies in the Fire Department bombarded the police with pleas on his behalf. The police held the man overnight and then released him the next day. His friends picked him up.

In the end, all that Margaret accomplished with the story was to complicate the investigation while trying to absolve Mike of kidnapping charges. It worked. Not only was it a good break, taking the spotlight off of Mike, but the rich young man was officially cleared.

Having dealt with the fire-captain lead, the detectives returned to their case with a nagging sense of dissatisfaction with Margaret's identification of the Willow River baby as baby Shirley Ann. Given the nurses' certainty that the dead baby lacked several characteristics of Margaret's baby, how could the mother, herself, not concur in their assessment? Could it be that the young mother had paid so little attention to her own newborn?

Later that same day, Margaret turned the investigation upside down yet again when she refuted her own story about the involvement of the fireman. She reverted to her original accusation: that Mike Osman was the baby's father, that he wanted the newborn drowned in Lake Calhoun, and that he had made good on that desire. Margaret claimed Mike really had kidnapped her baby. This time, to back up the charge, she gave Detectives Lehmeyer and Lindholm the name of a man who had seen Mike at General Hospital on August 4th, the day before the baby's disappearance.

By this time, however, Margaret had no credibility with the police. Lehmeyer and Lindholm did not believe anything she said. Besides, with ample family money, the Osmans were able to buy off the authorities, who never filed charges against Mike, not even for statutory rape. Indeed, the newspapers never acquired the last name of seventeen-year-old Mike. As the officials closed the case and filed away all of their police reports, the young man's last name was blacked out throughout the files, nearly everywhere. In page after page of investigative notes, court documents, and other reports and logs, his last name was gone, as if he never existed. It would have been impossible for anyone to ever find out the man's true identity were it not for one instance, a single document with a single word, "Osman," that happened by chance to survive the censor's pen. Regardless, the young Mike emerged from the scandal with his record incredibly clean. Charged only with immoral conduct, Mike gained his release with a one-thousand-dollar bond. He was off the hook for everything that he had done in Minneapolis, and in Willow River, for that matter.

# 11

## Sentence

Margaret had spent little time in school and lacked functional English skills. As a result, when the girl wanted to write a letter to Edward Goff, the assistant district attorney, a police matron essentially wrote it for her. On September 12th, the matron took dictation and helped Margaret to compose the following letter:

*Dear Mr. Goff,*

*I am writing this little extra note to apologize for the stories I have told you, and I hope you accept. I want you to feel toward me like you first did, but not the way you feel about me now. I think if we got Agnes, with you and I in your office, we could make her confess everything and then you will see that I am telling the truth. I wish that you would please ask the Judge if I can have another week stay, in hopes that this thing will all be cleared up and I would like to talk to you as soon as possible.*

After receiving no reply, the police matron helped Margaret write a second letter on September 17th:

*Dear Mr. Goff,*

*I am writing this little letter in hopes of clearing this whole thing. I would have told you everything and just how it happened today when I was down there, only I would have rather talked to you alone. Tuesday afternoon August 4th Mike and I were standing out in the hall at General Hospital, I told him that I did not want to go to the Maternity Home for three months. Later that same night about 8:30 I was standing in the hall looking out the window when Mike came up and talked to me, our conversation was about the baby, and Mike said that George would help to get it out of the hospital, and that him and George would take care of the baby.*

Margaret's last-minute appeals went nowhere. Like everyone else, the county attorney and Judge Bardwell had had enough. Although he had earlier said that he would give Margaret one last chance to talk to him before sending her to the Sauk Center Training School for Delinquent Girls, the judge changed his mind, determining that, since Margaret had already told so many conflicting stories, she had lost all credibility. The judge felt that Margaret could add nothing to the case that would have any credence, and he understood that Margaret was simply playing a delaying game. All she wanted was another postponement. But the judge was not in the mood to delay her sentencing again.

Though officials did not know what had become of the girl's baby, they did know that Margaret was an incorrigible and promiscuous juvenile, that she was likely involved in the baby's disappearance, and that she had said that the dead baby was hers. No one knew why Margaret said that, but she had. And she had to be punished for it

The reporter Eric Sevareid, who later became a popular CBS News commentator, later described his own investigation of the case.

*"I spent three weeks in Police Headquarters, in Washington Avenue saloons, in parlors of innumerable citizens trying to solve the celebrated local mystery of the missing baby, stolen from the bed of its fifteen-year-old unwed mother in the city hospital. I worked morning, noon, and night, uncovered various bits of evidence, and finally located a youthful suspect who police were convinced was the kidnapper, but whom they were unable to convict. I had always had the normal citizens' respect for the police, but during this experience discovered to my surprise that we reporters were frequently hours and days ahead of the police unraveling the mystery."*

The end of August neared. The baby had been missing for three weeks and the days continued to tick past, while the authorities were at a loss as to how to proceed with the case. In fact, the Hennepin county attorney admitted that the case had him completely baffled. On August 30th, the county attorney called in a Minneapolis psychiatrist, Doctor Michael, and asked him to examine Margaret.

A consultant, Dr. Michael was considered an authority in the field of psychiatry, and he had a particular expertise in the area of law enforcement. In fact, Dr. Michael was one of three psychiatrists appointed to examine Minnesota State Penitentiary inmates who were suspected of mental illness or deficiencies.

When he met with Margaret, the psychiatrist took the girl through the entire case, starting at the beginning and having Margaret retrace her steps. While the doctor tried to trip her up, Margaret smiled through the entire interview and never explained why she had changed her story so many times.

At the end of the session, the psychiatrist had copious notes and little else. He stated that, in some respects, Margaret was mentally alert, although in other respects she was far below normal. He also described her as "amoral," or as having no morals. To supplement this analysis, the psychiatrist visited the Bolin home to interview the girl's parents, and he questioned her cousin, Mrs. Clyde Peterson, and her aunt, Betsy Bolin. Then he questioned Margaret again. In his second examination of Margaret, Dr. Michael spent another two hours questioning her.

On September 2nd, the psychiatrist reported that Margaret was a "dull normal," with an IQ of eighty-eight. In his report, he also stated that Margaret had reverted to her original story—that she and Mike had given the baby to a nurse in blue, rather than letting Mike drown the baby in Lake Calhoun. The psychiatrist also said that, though Margaret showed no sign of psychosis or insanity, she had social moral values several years below her age. He explained that Margaret had become delinquent and, to shield herself, the girl always lied to her mother. The psychiatrist reported that Margaret had said that the reason for having the baby taken away was so that she could avoid the three-month period when she would be under the mandatory surveillance of the Minnesota Child Welfare League. Three weeks into the case, everyone was sick and tired of it. The investigation was going nowhere, but running them ragged. They were ready to be done with it.

Following the psychiatrist's report, Margaret anticipated sentencing. Perhaps in a late effort to show good faith, she made a final statement to Judge Waite in Minneapolis, clearing Mike's friend George of any wrongdoing. She also cleared Agnes of any involvement in the case.

Margaret's two-week temporary detention at the Girls' Home was about to expire.

Though they were dreadfully weary of the case, Detectives Lehmeyer and Lindholm hoped to get Margaret another two-week stay, during which they would give the case a last-ditch effort in the hopes that the additional weeks would provide enough time to solve the case. They went to the juvenile judge to get another stay, which they won.

# 12

## FINAL DISPOSITION

Up in Pine County, Sheriff Hannes Rypkema had wanted to investigate Mike Osman's involvement in the dead-baby case, but before he could proceed with that angle of inquiry, the Minnesota Bureau of Criminal Apprehension insisted that the sheriff turn all of his files over to them. After he did, everything was hushed up.

For the rest of his life, Sheriff Rypkema was haunted by the case of the infanticide of the Willow River baby. In his later years, as he spent winters in Arizona, the case still bothered him—not only because of the horror of seeing the dead baby, but because he was never able to close the case. The sheriff long believed that the facts of the case had been suppressed, that Mike Osman got preferential treatment from the police, and that Mike and Margaret got away with murder.

In 1936, as the case was deliberately abandoned, the Pine County newspaper ran the headline, "Dear God, Please, Have Someone Identify This Baby." The article referred to the baby as a "small mite of humanity," and called it the "most puzzling case in the annals of both city and county law enforcement agencies." Rightly, the paper surmised that the case "fairs to gather dust of the years as an unresolved mystery."

Indeed.

The townspeople of Willow River wondered why Margaret's family didn't claim the baby and have her buried, but the fact is that they didn't. The people of Finlayson raised a collection for a small white casket for the Willow River baby. Though they lived in the desperate poverty of the Great Depression, they also purchased a tiny dress in which the baby girl would be buried, so that she would be laid to rest in something other than a pillowcase.

North of Finlayson, the people of Willow River gathered on August 23th. They covered the casket in a summer sheer fabric with a pretty floral pattern. They gathered some flowers and carried the infant's casket, following the Reverend Eldon Sporleader in a little procession to the cemetery. Two ladies sang "Jesus Loves Me" and "Rock of Ages" as the residents of Willow River walked somberly to Potter's Field.

About eight blocks away from the island, in the river where the baby's body had been found in the black canvas bag, the three-week-old infant was laid to rest in an unmarked grave. Located at Sunnyside Cemetery, Section I, Lot 326, the small anonymous mound was surrounded by jack pines and scrub oaks.

Positively identified as Shirley Ann Bolin, the newborn was buried with compassion and dignity, but without a death certificate. Nor did she have a birth certificate, because she was not Shirley Ann Bolin.

Perhaps Margaret, too, was weary of the case. She indicated that she wanted to see her favorite aunt, Betsy Bolin, and to tell her the truth. Though Margaret met with her aunt, the girl gave Betsy no new information. Police brought Betsy into headquarters with Margaret's mother, Barbara. Detectives Lehmeyer and Lindholm interrogated the two women.

Everyone seemed to feel that Margaret was "shielding" someone. In any case, Margaret insisted that Mike and his friend, George, had given the baby to the nurse in blue in the hospital hallway, and that she never saw the infant after that. Since Mike was already officially in the clear for whatever reasons, no one put him in jail, and no one asked him about the nurse in blue. But they did have a new lead to follow.

Lehmeyer and Lindholm heard reports that a man had been seen hanging around Margaret's home in a 1929 Ford Coach automobile all summer and fall. The detectives went to the Bolin's home on 25th Avenue South to check it out. The man, Ted Plantenberg, owned the car and everything about him seemed to check out. The detectives never knew that Margaret had a little secret regarding Ted, who was never involved in the investigation, although he was another of Margaret's sexual partners.

Later in life, Ted Plantenberg was found dead under a bridge, his shoes missing. His relatives had never heard of Margaret Bolin—and there's little reason to think that they would have. After all, it was not uncommon for men to sit in their cars, parked near Margaret's house, the front passenger seats holding a bottle of perfume or another trinket to be traded to the pretty young girl in exchange for her sexual favors.

As the case was winding down, Margaret sent the detectives on another wild-goose chase, claiming that a woman named Lyla Peterson was with Mike when he took the baby. Lehmeyer and Lindholm chased down the lead and learned that Mike and a girlfriend named Lyla Peterson had been seen in several beer parlors in Minneapolis just before the disappearance of the baby from Minneapolis General Hospital. The investigators had learned that the woman had left Minneapolis at 6:20 PM on the day of the abduction, taking a bus to a cousin's home, where she stayed for a few days. Then, on August 22nd, the woman left Minnesota by car with some friends, heading for Helena, Montana. The police report, however, noted that Lyla Peterson hated Jews and did not "keep company with any Jew-born boys." Still, the police thoroughly investigated the lead.

The Minneapolis police sent a letter to the police in Helena, Montana, requesting information about Lyla Peterson. Eager to find out if the woman was an accomplice in the baby's kidnapping, Detectives Lehmeyer and Lindholm requested that the Helena police interview the woman and then advise them about the interview.

The investigators followed up the letter with a telegram to Helena's Chief of Police. In the telegram, they requested that the police chief advise them by telegram whether Lyla was living in Helena with her sister. They described Lyla as a stout young woman of about twenty-two years, with auburn hair, a twisted lower jaw, and a large lower lip. Lehmeyer and Lindholm requested that their letter be treated confidentially. They also asked that the Helena police try to investigate secretly whether or not Lyla had been accompanied by a baby girl, about a month old.

In response to this inquiry, the Minneapolis police received a telegram from the Helena, Montana, police, who stated that the girl in question was staying in Wick, Montana, a mining camp about twenty miles outside of Helena. To learn more information, the Helena police offered to drive out to Wick.

In yet another conversation, Margaret told Detectives Lehmeyer and Lindholm that this girlfriend of Mike's who had traveled to Helena, had taken the missing baby with her on August 5th.

The Hennepin county attorney dispatched Lehmeyer and Lindholm to Helena and, when they arrived, they thoroughly explored the case with the Helena Chief of Police. Lehmeyer and Lindholm learned that Lyla had never heard of Margaret or Mike, and she knew nothing about a missing baby. Since the woman might have known Mike by another name, the investigators thoroughly described his appearance to her. She stated positively that she did not know him. Further, Lyla Peterson told the Minneapolis investigators that she would gladly return to Minneapolis at her own expense if Minneapolis authorities wanted to question her.

Despite the woman's apparent honesty and her adamant statement, the two detectives, aided by the Helena Superintendent of Police, investigated Lyla Peterson for an entire day, checking on her movements and validating her information with others who knew her, primarily looking to determine whether anyone had seen her with a baby. Of all the friends, neighbors, and acquaintances that the detectives questioned, no one knew anything about Lyla caring for a baby. Having satisfied themselves that the lead was another dead end, the two detectives returned to Minneapolis.

On September 11, 1936, the judge committed Margaret to the Sauk Center Training School for Delinquent Girls, where she was to be confined until her eighteenth birthday. Since Margaret had not attended school since her early years at Jackson Grade School, the judge hoped that the girl's detention would be good for her, as she would finally have the opportunity to complete her high school education and earn her diploma.

This was the final disposition of the case. According to the record, the county attorney and the police dismissed the case on February 8, 1937, noting that according to Margaret Bolin, her baby was supposedly the one that was found dead at Willow River.

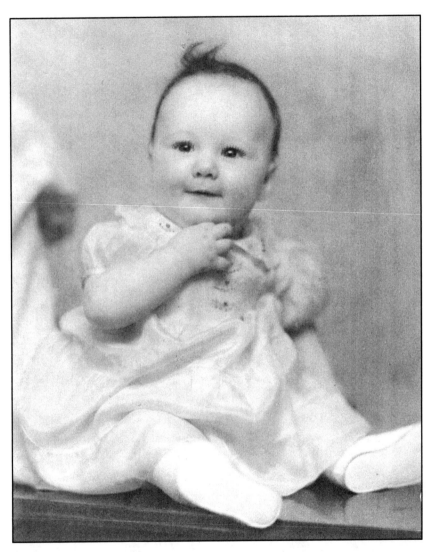

The author at six months old

Inga Sophie Reihdahl, age 25 (1931)

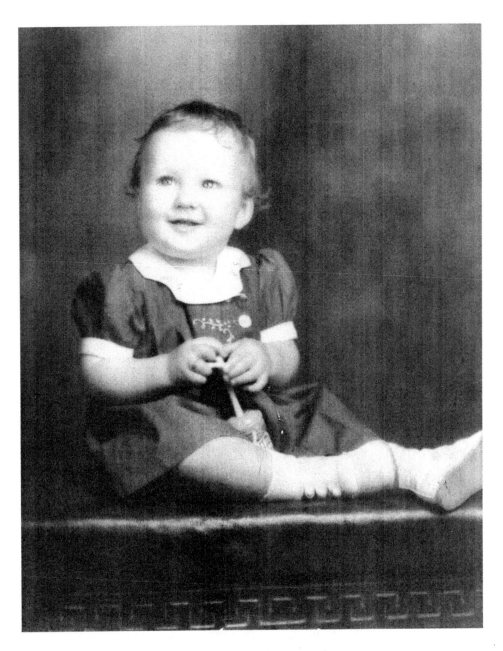

**The author at nine months**

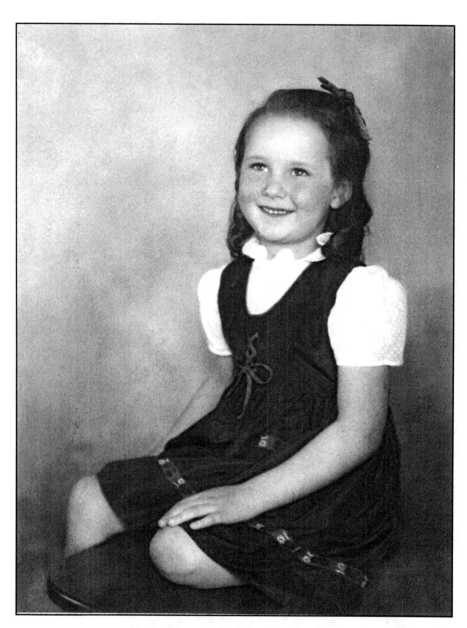

**First Day of Kindergarten, age 5**

**Margaret, 1942, after second daughter was born**

**Richard's graduation picture**
**1953**

**Lorene's graduation picture**
**1954**

**Lonnie's graduation picture**
**1972**

**Ronnie's graduation picture**
**1974**

**St. Patrick's Day**
**1971**

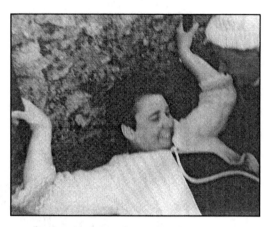

**Margaret at her mother's
house, 1974**

**Lorene kissing the
Blarney Stone, 1976**

**January 6, 1979
Seattle, WA**

**Lorene playing organ at St. Timothy Church, 1995**

**Lorene for church album, 2005**

# PART 2

## DOING THE RIGHT THING

# 13

## IRISHIN

I was born in Minneapolis, where both of my parents had jobs, even though it was the middle of the Depression. My father was a gas maker for the Minneapolis Gas Company, where he made sixty dollars a week—excellent pay during the Depression. He was a foreman who watched the gas pressure on the gauges and gas holders. My mother also worked, making about twenty-five dollars a week as a housekeeper in the nurses' dormitory at Minneapolis General Hospital. When I was born, Mother gave notice that she wanted to quit her job. She didn't get any maternity leave, so my parents drove with me to Wisconsin, where we stayed with my mother's family. Until my mother's notice was up, I stayed with my grandparents while my parents returned to Minneapolis to work. About a month later, my mother's notice was up so she quit her job and then the three of us were able to be together in Minneapolis.

When I was four years old, my parents bought a little white bungalow in northeast Minneapolis, in a suburb called Robbinsdale. I loved Robbinsdale. It was a new area where people moved to raise their children, and new houses were going up everywhere, all of them filled with growing families. Our house was in the newer section, about two blocks east of Victory Memorial Drive, which divided Minneapolis from Robbinsdale, and about two blocks west of Crystal Lake. Our house sat on a corner lot, wrapped by a sloping lawn, shaded by trees, and surrounded by playmates in every direction. I had so many friends my age to play with, and that's all I did.

My best friend was Joan Streeter, but she moved away before we started kindergarten. The Beckstroms moved in and their daughter Barbara became my new best friend, but we knew dozens of kids: Molly Lee, Jeannie, Janet, Patricia, Bobby, Dickey, Jerome, and so many more. Once in a while, squabbles with other children would get out of hand so, in case anybody was mean to us, Barbara and I would carry a piece of clothesline and a stick. One day, after my mother washed and curled my hair, Barbara and I went out to play in the sandbox. Before long, Bobby dumped a pail of sand on my freshly-coiffed head. As he turned to run, I swatted him with my clothesline across his back. Later that day, Bobby's mother came to our house and complained to my parents about me, since my retaliation with the clothesline rope had left a mark on Bobby's back. My parents couldn't believe it, because Bobby was a lot bigger than I was. No matter. The next day we were all friends again.

Barbara and I couldn't wait to start kindergarten. When I was five years old, my mother used my baptismal certificate to enroll me in kindergarten at Twin Lake Grade School, which was in the Robbinsdale

School District. A three-story schoolhouse, it included kindergarten through the fifth grade. Mother bought me a silk jumper, which I wore with a dotted-Swiss top, and she took my picture in the outfit as I got ready for my first day of school. Barbara and I buttoned up our teddy-bear coats, picked up our lunch boxes, and walked down the alley to meet the bus a block away. I loved school. We only attended for half of the day, and we had such fun playing games and skipping rope during recess. Since we wore teddy-bear coats, we played "Bear" at recess. As hunters, the boys would try to catch us, and I would come home with torn sleeves all the time.

After school, Barbara and I loved to play "big lady," dressing up in our mothers' old dresses from the 1930s and clomping around in pairs of high heels, or sometimes spectator pumps. We had endless fun, pretending that we were grown-ups and thinking that we were big deals.

Though both of my parents were Norwegian, I would tell the other children that I was "Irishin," meaning Irish. Since nearly everyone I knew was Scandinavian and I didn't know any Irish people, I have no idea where that came from, but I used to say it all the time. Apparently, I thought that I was Irish.

I could sit for hours in my swing under the oak tree, just singing. I loved music. So, when I was five years old, my mother inherited some money and bought me a piano. Right away, I started piano lessons. I was a natural at it and progressed quickly, while my mother showered me with encouragement. Music became my life and my parents were very proud of my musical accomplishments, which would grow throughout my life. I would become an excellent church organist, wedding pianist, singer, and choir director.

I loved going to Sunday School, where I sang in the "cherub" choir with other Sunday School children. I made so many new friends in Sunday School, and it was a wonderful part of my childhood. I especially loved the Christmas and Easter programs, in which I always sang solos. I sang for my uncle's funeral when I was five and I also became a church soloist, thanks to my mother's encouragement

Barbara and I loved taking the streetcar downtown with our mothers, who would take us clothes shopping or to the movies. Radio City Music Hall was our favorite theater because all of the movies came out there first. We loved Betty Grable, June Havor, Dan Dailey, and John Payne. When Betty Grable, June Havor, and John Payne starred in *The Dolly Sisters*, the movie became our favorite. Like all little girls, we daydreamed about being in the movies.

As much as I enjoyed outings with my mother and girly games with Barbara, I was a daddy's girl. My father was a wonderful man. Tall, with a good build and thin greying hair, he always wore beautiful suits with a vest and a matching tie. Like my mother, he loved children and always expected me to be a good girl. Every afternoon, I would sit in my swing and watch for him coming home from work, and, as soon as I saw him, I would run to meet him and carry his lunch pail. Every Friday was payday and, every Friday, he spoiled me with a Payday candy bar inside his lunch pail.

On Saturdays, my father and I did the grocery shopping together because my mother hated grocery shopping. Daddy and I would go to the supermarket, meat market, and bakery, and it was so much fun for me. When we got home, I'd often go grocery shopping with Barbara and her parents. I guess I liked grocery shopping!

Really, I liked doing anything and everything that I could do with my dad. He bought me a BB gun, which was only loaded when I was with him. I never used it like a toy, but took it along when we went pheasant hunting. My mother also got me a pair of jodhpurs and a matching jacket, which I wore for hunting. Sometimes, I'd pretend to be roasting a pheasant, bringing home a large bouquet of dried weeds that I'd present to my mother, and she would put them in the oven, which was unlit of course.

Daddy and I also went fishing together. Since we lived just two blocks from Crystal Lake, my father would often take me there to fish, and I would get so excited because I loved being in a boat on the water. But I wanted no part of swimming. Even though I went to swimming lessons, I never did learn how. I was afraid to get in the water.

Living so close to the lake, I saw five children drown. Crystal Lake was not a lake for swimming, but often, boys that I knew would go out in the water and get into trouble, and not make it back in. I remember the rowboats that went out on the water, dragging huge grappling hooks on the bottom of the lake, looking for the bodies. They found them. After seeing drowned bodies, I could not bring myself to try to swim.

Otherwise, I was pretty adventurous and independent. When Barbara and I were about seven years old, both of our mothers worked and we were trusted to take care of ourselves.

Though our mothers taught us not to get in anybody's car even if we knew them, and to keep the house doors locked, we were very grown-up for our ages. We walked all over town, rode our two-wheeled bikes, and we were even old enough to take the streetcar downtown by ourselves. I loved the streetcars—the noise of the tracks and the bright yellow colors—and Barbara and I liked to people-watch, which was always great on the streetcar. And taking the trip by ourselves, we thought we were really big deals!

We went to a big, downtown dime store and bought a ring and earring set with cheap yellow stones in them, and then we went to the movies at the Radio City Music Hall. We were in heaven. After the movies, we went to the Mayflower doughnut shop where I'd get a Pepsi and an orange-flavored doughnut with heavy frosting. Those doughnuts were out of this world. When we got on the streetcar to go home, ladies looked at us and said, "Those little girls should not be wearing jewelry." Since we recognized that they were just idle gossipers, we didn't care. We just stuck our noses up in the air. It was our first trip on the streetcars alone and we thought we were sensational.

One year, Barbara's cat had kittens and she got to keep one. She named her kitten Bubblegum. I just had to have one, but my parents said no. I couldn't stand it so, one afternoon, I brought one home—a little tiger kitten that I named Petunia. My kitty was so cute that my parents just couldn't make me give her back, and I was so happy! For weeks, when Barbara and I would get together to play, we'd bring Petunia and Bubblegum so they could visit each other. It was so fun! In the summers, my parents planned our annual vacations with family in Wisconsin, but I wanted to stay in Robbinsdale and play with my friends. When I was eight, we were about to leave but I was nowhere to be found, and my dad spent two hours looking for me. When he found me, he wasn't happy, but he took it in stride and I got a strong lecture before I climbed into the backseat of the car with Petunia.

My dad made a little leash for Petunia so that the cat could come everywhere with me. When we went into restaurants, Petunia was welcome and everyone doted on the cat. They even gave it some food and milk. But they all chuckled about the name, since it was a boy cat. I just didn't know it!

We finally arrived at my grandparents' farm, which seemed like another world to a city girl like me. My great-grandparents had homesteaded the land in the 1800s and, when I grew up, my grandparents, Ole and Lena Reindahl, still managed the dairy farm.

As soon as we got there, all the relatives came to greet us and we had a big picnic. All my cousins came, and we started to play, so before long, I was okay about being away from Robbinsdale. Every summer, I had such a good time playing with all my cousins—and there were a lot of them. Many were near my age and several were girls, so my cousins and I became the best of friends. Beverly and I were the same age so we have always been closest, but we also enjoyed Leroy and Lavern, who were a little older, Alan who was about the same age as us, and the younger children: Diann, Delores, Linda, Gail, Bonnie, Patty, Philip, George, Larry, Bruce, and Lavon. From sunrise to sunset and into the evening, I always had plenty of children to play with. Rooted and established in love, we played together from morning until night. We grew up knowing that we were precious to Jesus and to our families, and we believed that, whatever we were doing, our parents, grandparents, aunts, and uncles were always close, keeping a watchful eye on us.

My grandparents' dairy farm covered eighty acres, about half forest and half orchard, with apples, pears, and plums. In addition to cats and dogs, they had lots of farm animals like cows, chickens, and pigs. I loved climbing trees, helping to feed the cows, digging up potatoes, and picking wildflowers. Most of all, I loved picking wild strawberries, which we'd use to make strawberry shortcake. Sometimes,

Grandmother would take us to visit her friend, Mrs. Brihn, a neighbor up the road who always gave us cookies with lemonade.

My aunts and uncles often entertained us, inviting us over to their homes for dinner or a picnic, and my parents often reciprocated by inviting them to our vacation cottage. The best party was on the Fourth of July, when the town put on a small carnival with a polka band, dancing, and fireworks. Everyone in the family loved listening to the polka band, and I was in heaven, since I liked any kind of music. My parents would usually dance to a couple of songs, just for the fun of it, and I always thought that it was so funny to see them dance together. That may have been partly because my dad always teased my mother about her dancing, saying that she needed more rhythm in her feet and less in her body!

When we got back to Robbinsdale, I couldn't wait to get back into my city life. I got together with all of my friends and we walked to the movie theater for the kids' matinée on Saturday afternoons. We cheered for the good guys and booed the bad guys. Though we watched a lot of westerns with Roy Rogers and Gene Autry, Barbara and I loved the musicals. We learned all the songs in the movie musicals that we saw, and loved to sing them, on and on. We even put on musicals in our basements, inviting all the neighborhood children to come and making money by selling popcorn and ice-cube-tray popsicles.

Since there was always new construction going on around our neighborhood, we became friends with the tradesmen, especially the electricians. They would give us the slugs—the round metal 9in-sized discs, which they drilled out of electrical boxes, which we loved. Slugs worked in all the vending machines, so they were as good as cash for us kids. When they changed the vending machines so that they wouldn't accept slugs, we were so disappointed.

I had the biggest disappointment when I was eleven, in 1947. That was the year when my dad retired and we had to move to Wisconsin. My father had promised his brother that, when he retired, we would move up to take over the family farm. We were going to Wisconsin, and this time, it wasn't just a summer vacation. Both of my parents were giving up good jobs, but when my dad made a promise, it was his word. As much as Mother and I tried to talk Daddy out of the move, he was committed to living up to his promise.

My dad was a good man. When he made a decision, he stuck by it, and he was as kind as he was determined. A godly man, my father was good-hearted, always ready to help anyone. He was a give-you-the-shirt-off-his-back kind of man, who would lend money to relatives and act charitably in any situation. One time, we were in church when a man who lived near us and attended our church robbed our house and took jewelry and trinkets. Saying that the man must have needed money very badly, my father refused to call the police, though my mother and I begged him to report the theft. During the next weeks, I saw the man's daughter wearing my jewelry in church and, at times, I would see her with some of the other things that had been stolen from us. My dad told me not to say anything, but, boy, that was hard! That's the kind of man my father was.

My mother and I both wanted to stay in Minneapolis, where we enjoyed going to our favorite Chinese restaurant, traveling downtown on the streetcar, and walking to matinées on Saturdays. We loved living in the big city and couldn't bear to leave it. And I was sick at losing my school, neighborhood, friends, and everything else that I loved about Robbinsdale. As a little girl, moving to the farm for good was very hard to do.

Barbara and I cried.

In school, every Friday had been "bank day," when we would bring in our change and deposit the money in our bank accounts. Before I moved, I had to go to the big bank downtown to get my money and close my account. I cried again. As I collected my own money, I felt as though my whole world was being taken away from me.

Soon, the moving truck came. It was a Saturday and my friends came to say goodbye while I sat in my swing and cried. It was almost more than I could bear, but everything got loaded into the truck and, before long, it was time to get in the car. I continued to cry as I cuddled with Petunia on the drive down Victory Memorial Drive, away from my home, away from my world. Trying to comfort me, my dad said, "It will be okay." But I knew that it would never be the same, and it wasn't.

I was a year ahead of my Wisconsin class and the school wanted me to skip a year. But I was already almost a year younger than my classmates and my parents would not allow me to skip, so I sat and read library books for the entire school year. As I longed for my classmates and friends in Robbinsdale, that year was the first of two terrible, unhappy years.

Everyone in my class wrote to me every week and Barbara and I always wrote to each other. While I looked forward to the letters, it wasn't the same as being home in Minneapolis. Mother and I made frequent trips back to shop and visit friends, and that helped.

I found comfort in church and music, and it helped that my cousin Beverly was in my class. At least I had one friend. But, even for my father, Wisconsin wasn't what he thought it would be. He missed his buddies in Minneapolis, though they visited often. And he never complained about life on the farm, though it was a challenge for him after living in Minneapolis for so long. He had lost his instinct for farming and had to learn about it all over again.

My mother took a job as a seamstress for a dry cleaner, doing clothing alterations, and she seemed to like to work endlessly. To help out, I did all the housework and helped with the cooking. Mother liked both of us to have nice clothes and I was always very well dressed. She also liked to have nice things around the house, and she and I used to enjoy looking at magazines like House Beautiful and Better Homes and Gardens, appreciating the decor of the beautiful homes.

Since it was a farming community, our nearest neighbor was about three blocks down the road. I always felt disgusted when I saw men wearing bib overalls covered with cow manure, and I saw that all the time. As I started making friends, it was hard for me because the kids were so different from my city friends. The young people near the farm had never ridden a streetcar or seen Minneapolis. Instead, they were interested in cows, pigs, and 4H. At least they had the Girl Scouts, which was something that I loved. I always sold more cookies than anyone else and invested myself in the projects, such as learning first aid, visiting a homeless shelter, and building friendships with all the girls in the troop.

Of course, we found a new church. We joined my mother's childhood church and also went to the church that my father had attend-ed. Though I was used to our big-city church and the children's choir, participating in the music programs at church helped me adjust to Wisconsin, and I continued to sing, in the choir as well as performing as a soloist. I always took music and voice lessons to achieve my goals, and at the age of twelve, I became a church organist.

Unlike Minneapolis, in Wisconsin I was surrounded by family. From time to time, I heard things—gossipy comments—that I had been adopted. I sometimes wondered about what I'd heard but I knew that I had such wonderful parents that the stories could not be true. Normally, I dismissed what I'd heard as the idle gossip of people who didn't have enough to do. But, then, one time, I saw a woman looking at me and I heard her say the word, "adopted," under her breath. I couldn't let it go and decided to ask my mother about it. She seemed to tense up a bit as she looked away from me. "Is that what she said?" Mother would say, trying to sound casual. "I cannot imagine where anybody would get that idea!" After her dismissal of it, I also dismissed the rumor as silly. But I remembered that she seemed a little anxious while we talked about it.

Every year, we went to the big Minneapolis Gaslight Company picnic with my father's former colleagues and friends. The company held the all-day picnic at a permanent amusement park at Lake Excelsior, a Minneapolis suburb. I always teamed up with my friend, Margie Krieger, whose dad had worked with mine. We loved all the goodies, roller-coaster rides, and other fun. I was about fourteen in 1950, when we went to the picnic and my dad's former company tried to convince him to come back to work at the gas company. He considered it, and was tempted, but he decided to stay on the farm in Wisconsin. Mother and I were so disappointed!

That same year, I finally started high school. Music continued to be my focus, and I sang as a soloist as well as in the school choir and glee club, and played the French horn in the concert band, marching band, and pep band. Competing as a soloist, I won many awards. I had a wonderful music teacher who gave me voice lessons and coached me for competition. In addition to all the music I played in school, I played the organ in church for services as well as funerals and weddings. Music was my savior. Without music and church, I don't think that I could have handled the move.

One Sunday in church, I overheard some people talking. "If she's adopted," I heard, "why don't they tell her?" I assumed that they were talking about me but I couldn't be sure. I learned that a family in our church had a daughter who had given up a baby for adoption around the time that I was born, and there was some gossip that I was that baby. I recognized that I did not look much like my relatives but, then again, I didn't look like that other woman, either. Thinking about it, I considered that no one in my family was musically inclined, as I certainly was. But, in the end, I took it as silly gossip.

I had many friends in high school. As a baton twirler, my cousin Beverly was in the band and we were close. Phyllis was another great friend and we spent lots of time together. The three of us were part of the "Big Nine," which is what we called our group of nine girlfriends. Like most high school kids, we thought we were the greatest! We hung out together during lunch and at all of our school's sporting events.

I loved playing in the pep band at basketball games and the marching band at football games. Student admission was fifty cents but I got into the games for free, so three of my girlfriends would curl up in the trunk of my car to sneak in. As I pulled into the parking lot, the teacher who was taking tickets would say, "I see you're alone tonight, Lorene." When I parked in the band parking area,

I'd open the trunk and my friends would giggle as they climbed out, feeling silly.

I met my husband when both of us were in high school, in 1953. He attended an opposing school. Beverly and I were in my parents' 1950 Ford and I was driving, following Richard's car.

I passed him going ninety miles an hour and then eased up on my speed. He passed my car and drove on, and then waited for us at the malt shop. Richard and his friend Jack commenced to acting like idiots, as boys will, to get our attention. Richard definitely got mine! That was the beginning of a serious case of puppy love. Six months later, we really fell in love, and in 1954, we were married.

Richard's mother was one of the women in town who thought that I was adopted. One time, I attended a family wedding with Richard. A guest at the wedding introduced me to his wife as his cousin, as a joke. My mother-in-law and others seemed to think that I resembled a certain woman, who they thought was my mother. I didn't think I resembled her at all. My mother-in-law had also heard that I was related to a family that was very active in our church. Whenever I asked my mother about such talk, she said it was not true.

# 14

# MOTHER

I was an adult woman with children of my own before my mother told me her secret—her secret about me. I could not process it. It was incomprehensible, and it plunged me into a nightmare. And though I began that day in May, 1967, worried about my mother, that concern would be infused with irony by the end of that day.

It started as a beautiful morning, but I had one troubling concern on my mind. At sixty-one years of age, my mother had been widowed for a dozen years. She was about to remarry, but the man who would become my stepfather was an abusive alcoholic, a vulgar slob with a criminal record. About sixty years old, George was an average-looking man with a medium build, ruddy complexion, and brown hair that was just getting streaked with grey. Whenever I saw him, he was clean and well-kept enough in a cotton shirt and cotton work pants, but his alcoholism was obvious. A lifetime of that kind of abuse shows through.

It showed in his family, as well. George had fathered four children with his first wife and, after he wiped out all of her assets, she had him jailed many times for non-support. She hated him, as did most of his children. He had gone through the fortunes of several women and it seemed my mother was next.

The last time I had seen George, he was (of course) drunk. He used vulgar language in front of my husband, my two sons, and me. We were appalled. In our family, we never swore or used vulgar language. My parents raised me not to swear, drink, or smoke, and so when George behaved the way he did, I took my family and left immediately, without even saying good-bye. To think that this horrible man was going to marry my mother! I was sick about it.

Mother and I discussed it over the phone many times. My relatives were calling me all the time, asking me to put a stop to the marriage, so nearly every day, I called her, asking if she had "gotten rid of that drunk yet." She hadn't, so I pleaded with her time and again to change her mind.

Over and over, I reminded her of what a wonderful man my father had been. A God-fearing father and husband, Daddy's life revolved around his family and his church. We had never missed a Sunday. And here she was, about to marry a man whose drinking was the priority in his life. On the phone, she responded by saying that it was no fun to be alone. I understood this and agreed with her, but I insisted that she find a man who worshiped God and attended church. It didn't work. My telephone ultimatums went nowhere.

I realized that Mother was dead serious about marrying George and I was disgusted that I couldn't talk any sense into her. I decided that I needed to have a showdown with her, to appeal to her in person.

So on that beautiful day in May, my husband and I piled our sons into our new Ford and drove ninety miles, from our home in Bloomington, Minnesota to my mother's house in Amery, Wisconsin. It was a long, somber drive, as I steeled myself for what I had to do.

A typical Midwest town with frame houses and shade trees, Amery was warm and sunny when we reached my mother's neighborhood in the mid-morning. A recently developed section at the edge of town, my mother's area had new roads, sidewalks, and buildings that were clean and fresh with new paving and new paint. My mother, in fact, had waited for the builders to finish so she could move into the new apartment

Richard pulled the car to the curb in front of my mother's building. A handsome man, he kept himself in shape and dressed well, wearing his hair short. As I said goodbye, my husband leaned close to me and I could smell his Polo aftershave and cologne as he gave me a supportive pat on my shoulder with a well-worn hand. We said goodbye and then he drove off. They were driving a dozen miles down the road to visit Richard's brother so that I could I speak to my mother alone.

My mother's building stood next to the road, its eight apartments distributed between two floors. Wearing Loden green cotton slacks with a matching green knit top, I walked up the stairs.

I could smell the coffee aroma coming from my mother's apartment. I was physically frail at that time—ill with colitis—and I was quite underweight, so I pulled my body up the stairs as I looked up to the top of the steps. As usual, my mother was eager to see me, and she stood holding open the front door and its storm screen, waiting for me. Though my dark ash brown hair was cut in a short, Sassoon style, my bangs tickled my forehead and I brushed a wisp of hair aside as I looked up at her.

"Hi, Mother," I said, smiling as I looked at her with my green eyes. I reached my arms around her plump body before I pulled back to look at her, appreciating the cute red print that she wore over tan slacks. She looked very put-together, as usual. "You're wearing the blouse I gave you!"

"Yes," she smiled." It's pretty, isn't it?" At sixty-one years of age, she looked more like fifty, with short curled dark brown hair and sparkling blue eyes. "You like that locket, don't you?" she observed, adding, "I'm glad you always wear it."

"Yes," I said softly. "I love it."

My mother had given me the beautiful gold locket, which hung on a long chain and held pictures of me when I was about six months old. Other than that and my wedding rings, I didn't wear any jewelry. "How are you, Renie?" she asked, closing the screen but leaving the door open as we walked into her apartment. She knew my colitis had been very bad recently.

Though we tried to be as warm as we usually were with each other, she knew why I was there and the air was tense between us. She had decorated the apartment with her usual flair, buying new furniture to go with her early American motif. She had a new sofa and matching chair in a woven green and gold floral fabric, and a recliner in a complementary reddish brown. Her new, wood-grain dinette table was surrounded by green floral chairs, and the table was covered with a cloth in a small green print. With her antiques adding to the mix, her apartment was very homey and comfortable, and yet lovely.

"I'm okay," I sighed, looking around the apartment as I dropped my big black handbag in a corner. Thank goodness George was not there. If he had been, I would have left. I'm sure that he knew that I was coming and why, and she had arranged for him to be somewhere else.

Being Norwegian, my mother made her coffee good and strong, and she poured me a cup as we sat and talked at the kitchen table. I flavored my coffee with powdered creamer and noticed the plate of cake and raised-glazed doughnuts, which she'd obviously just bought at the bakery. She took a doughnut and dunked it into her black coffee, as I helped myself to a doughnut as well.

We started with small talk, chatting about our health, the weather, my work as an accountant and news about family and friends. Despite the tension between us, we always carried on good conversations. We discussed her youngest sister, who didn't have a very good marriage, and Mother asked about my dear friend, Barb. Of course, she also wanted to know about the boys and what they were up to. And she talked about coming to my house so I could give her a perm, cut, and color, which I routinely did for her and everyone in the family.

Though I normally enjoyed catching up with her, on this day, I had other issues on my mind, so I was friendly but cool. After our many phone conversations, she knew exactly how I felt, and I wanted to get around to the reason I came, but it is easier to be forceful and direct over the telephone than in person. Distracted by the sounds of cars going by on the highway outside, I could also hear birds chirping outside and squirrels frolicking in the trees. I watched my mother, and then the words came to me.

I am a soft-spoken person, but also very direct. I was also extremely nervous and quite ill, so it took everything I had to bluntly change the subject, but it was the purpose of the visit. "You're not going to marry that drunk, are you?"

"Yes," was her simple reply.

Though my voice was strong, I felt desperately weak. "Mother," I said, "do not marry him. You will live to regret it. After all, he spent all of his first wife's money and now he just needs another patsy so he can keep drinking without having to work!"

"It's no fun to live alone," Mother said softly.

"I understand," I said. "But a vulgar alcoholic is not the right choice for you."

"But he has nowhere to go," she said, trying to persuade me. "Besides, he's a changed man." She spoke softly, though I could see that she was getting agitated and I could tell that she felt sorry for him, that she believed that he was capable of changing. Sick to my stomach, I felt only dread that my mother was determined to marry a man who was the exact opposite of my father. George had been that way all of his life, living always in saloons and bars.

"Mother," I said, "the last time we saw him, he was drunk and vulgar. He has not changed."

"Well, he's going to change," she persisted. "He's going to quit drinking."

Since my mother always wanted me to be a part of her life, she would never tell me to butt out, and I know that she took my position very seriously. I just couldn't live with myself if I had simply let well enough alone.

But we were getting nowhere. She knew how I felt, and I knew I only had one option left. "If you go through with this marriage," I said, trembling, "you will never see me or your grandchildren again.

I will not expose my family—my children—to a man like that." Serious and determined, nervous and sad, I said it with all the conviction and strength I had, and though I know my voice was weak, I was determined, and she had to have known that. I didn't know how to be more firm, how to convince her that I meant what I said because I was looking out for her well-being.

Though she knew that I would never accept him, she tried to act as if it was no big deal. "George and I have set a wedding date," she said solemnly. "And we want you there." This retort was her declaration that they were getting married, regardless of my ultimatum. She was dead serious, and I believe that she thought that I would give in and go along with the wedding. She and George had already made all the arrangements for the ceremony at a church, followed by a dance, and she was desperate for me and my family to attend. Her facial expression begged me to be at her wedding, to be part of her life. Though it was her way of telling me that she was serious, I think she also thought that I would relent and show up.

I desperately wanted to be part of my mother's life but, from then on, her life would include George, and I just couldn't do it. We both stood our ground and found ourselves at a standoff.

I got to a point when I felt too ill to fight her, and by then, I didn't much care what she did. I felt bad that she was making such a horrible mistake, but I also felt that there was nothing left to say because, no matter what I said or threatened, the wedding would go on. Since all of her wedding plans were made, I quickly realized the inevitability of the marriage. The situation seemed hopeless.

The mood between us was so strained that I couldn't wait to leave, and wished that Richard and the boys would walk through the door. I reiterated that we would not attend. Further, if she invited us for a Sunday dinner, we would not come if George was to be there. I told her I was serious, that I did not want to expose my sons to someone like him, not then and not ever. I knew, given my special bond with my mother, that I would never lose her, but I meant what I said.

She knew this was the truth.

A look of determination came over my mother's face. She knew that she could keep on insisting that my family and I come to her wedding, but deep down she had to have realized that I wouldn't. She rose from the table and walked five feet across the kitchen to the sink, standing with her back to me as she started washing dishes. Looking out the window in the opposite direction, I lifted my coffee cup to my lips, shaking as I took a small sip. I loved my mother very much, and I had never defied her. Putting the cup down, I almost dropped it onto the saucer. My mind was blank as I looked out on the oak trees and sipped coffee.

Ten minutes must have passed, with only the sound of the outdoors and the water in the sink as she washed dishes. When she finally spoke, her voice remained soft but I could hear the agitation in it. She sounded as if she needed to clear her throat. Standing perfectly still, she tried to talk, clearing her throat and speaking slowly, softly. Her voice was full of love.

"There's something that I think that you should know," she said, still washing dishes with her back to me." I think you should know that I'm not your real mother."

"What do you mean," I barely whispered, "you're not my real mother?"

"I saved your life," she said, with her back to me as she continued to wash her dishes with gentle hands. Her back was perfectly still, her head didn't move, and all I heard was the infrequent and muffled clinking of her nice china under the sudsy water in her sink.

I looked at my mother's back and then turned to look out the window. I was stunned, shocked. I did not understand and certainly did not grasp that her words had anything to do with me, with my reality. I felt forlorn—not angry, not upset, not agitated. Just lost. I could not speak.

"Your mother was only fifteen years old when she had you," my mother explained, as if she was talking to the wall above her sink. "I think that they called your father Mike. Your teenage mother and father were going to drown you in Lake Calhoun. I was just a short way down the hallway at Minneapolis General Hospital when I overheard them talking about this, and I went over to them quickly and said 'Please, don't do that. Let me have her!'

"They said that I had to get you out of the hospital before August 6th if I wanted you," she continued." So, I took you out on the 5th, at five o'clock in the morning. I got to you just in time. As I was taking you down the elevator, your teenage father and his friend were coming up the granite stairs, carrying a black canvas bag that they were going to drown you in. But I got you instead." I could hear the love in her voice, and also the seriousness. In a way, it was her usual tone, nothing dramatic, but the truth that she told me was dramatic beyond imagining.

"You can give me credit for one thing," she said. Her voice was soft and sweet, though full of determination while she continued to wash dishes with her back to me. "I loved you enough to save your life. From the minute I held you, I loved you as my own daughter." I believe that my mother thought that I would understand that she had saved my life, and that my gratitude for what she did, my appreciation for the beautiful childhood she'd given me, and my lifelong love for her, would change my feelings about her marriage to George. I think she thought that I would be so grateful that I would show my gratitude by accepting him and attending her wedding after all.

But, for me, in that moment, George did not matter in the least. I was too shocked to think about him or about anything else and, besides, I had already stated my case and my decision. But at that point, my mood had changed completely. George wasn't important anymore. I couldn't talk, and I just wanted Richard. I wanted to tell him what my mother had told me about myself—that my loving, wholesome, beautiful childhood was not real, that I was not Norwegian, and Mother and Daddy were not my real parents. But Richard wasn't there, and I was too ill, physically, to react in any way. I simply sat at the dinette table and gazed out the window, stunned.

I know that my mother did not want to hurt me, and she had tried not to. All she wanted was for me to love her. I always would, of course, but since I was holding dear to my values about George and the wedding, she was worried that I would not remain a big part of her life, and she did not want us to have this rift. She just wanted me to love her, as I always had, and she thought that by telling me how I had come to be her daughter, that I would see how much she loved me. I did. But I had never, ever doubted her love for me. Mother and I had always had a special bond. Even when I was a teenager, we would cuddle on the couch while we listened to the radio. I knew that our relationship was special and that it always would be, no matter what, but this was more devastating than anything I ever could have imagined.

Shocked and stunned by my mother's words, I was speechless. Starting to shake all over, I know that I had a look of horror on my face. I felt numb and confused, mentally crippled for the first time in my life. I felt as if I were in a dream, as if it weren't true after all. I trembled. After about ten minutes, some questions formed in my mind, and I calmed down enough to formulate them.

Looking at my mother's back as she kept washing dishes, I shivered. "What was my real mother's name?" I asked, my voice a shaky whisper.

She still did not turn to look at me. "Her name was Margaret Bolin," she answered quietly, with control and deliberation in her voice. "And the young man's name was Mike."

"Do I look like them?"

"You look like your mother."

"What nationality am I?"

"Irish," she replied.

"What happened to them?"

"Margaret was sent to a reform school—and she deserved it," said Mother. "I don't know what became of Mike."

I wondered what had happened to them and where they were, and I wondered why my real mother had wanted to drown me. I felt like screaming, but I never dealt with problems by having outbursts.

I kept my composure and silently started to pray. A person of deep faith, I believed that God was with me and would walk with me as I coped with my new view of myself, my family, my life. I prayed that God would help me get through this. I had no idea what I was in for, but I had always believed that God never gives us more than we can handle. In my case, though, I felt that he came very close.

My mother finally turned around. She carried the percolator over to the table and filled my gold and white Noritake cup with coffee. She poured herself a cup, too. Sitting at the table with me, she gave me another cake doughnut.

Suddenly, the apartment door opened and Richard and the boys walked in. My mother turned to look at them and then quickly smiled at me. Awkwardly, I walked to the door, not really to let them in but to be near Richard. When they entered the room, the mood lightened and everyone seemed somewhat happy, except for me. I gave Richard a quick kiss and then my tears started to flow. I couldn't keep the tears from running down my cheeks. Although Richard had known that I was going to have a showdown with my mother about her plans to marry George, as soon as he saw me he could tell that something else was very wrong.

Walking back to the table, I glanced at the kitchen sink and saw that my mother must have washed about a dozen dishes twenty-five times or more. Still, she acted as though nothing had happened. She had a nurturing look on her face and greeted my husband and children with joy and love, as she always did. My mother talked to Richard about his work and asked my sons about their summer vacations and what they were doing with their time, while the aroma of scalloped potatoes and ham filled the apartment. She went to the oven and pulled out the red Hall Sundial casserole that she had used all my life.

"Lunch is ready," Mother announced, expecting us to join her at the table. "I'm not hungry," I said. "I don't think we'll stay to eat."

Richard and the boys were very hungry so they shot down that idea, and I had to stay. Mother always cooked for us and always expected us to stay and dine, but I just could not imagine doing so. Everything seemed to be normal for everyone else, but it was not normal for but me. I was in a fog, overloaded, while Mother served the ham and potatoes as well as sandwiches and Jell-O for dessert. I don't remember eating any of it.

Finally, I left the kitchen and looked out the window, and then I went out to the patio. I stood there and stared into space. My brain seemed dead and I felt very ill.

When Richard was done eating, he joined me outside and I told him that I needed to go home. I was as white as a sheet and Richard knew that I was sick. He saw that he had to get me out of there, so he agreed to take me home right away. We went inside and prepared to leave.

Mother hugged everyone goodbye and, when it was my turn, she hugged me. "I love you so much," she said, giving me a kiss.

"I love you, too," I said.

"Don't forget to call me, Renie," she said.

The ninety-mile drive home seemed like an eternity. I desperately needed to tell Richard what had happened, but I was not ready to share it with my sons. In shock, I rode in silence, gazing at the countryside out the windows as the children chattered in the back seat. I wondered how my life could have been so wonderful that morning and so intensely painful now. I believed that my mother told me the truth so that I would feel grateful enough to stop my campaign to prevent her marriage to George. I thought about my childhood, how my mother had taught me to be afraid of kidnappers and never to talk to strangers or get into anyone's car. Crying some of the time, I reminisced about what a wonderful mother she was to me, and what a great grandmother she was to my sons.

Finally, we reached home. The boys went off to play with friends and Richard and I were finally alone. Desperately sad, I broke down, crying as I told Richard what my mother had said. As I formed her story into words of my own, I felt as though I were talking about somebody else—a stranger or a character in a story—as if it were a fantasy or a crazy bad dream, as if I were saying something that somehow wasn't true. *God, why me?* I thought.

Richard put his arms around me and held me tight, and then he pulled back to look at my face, streaked with tears. "I don't care where you came from," he said. "I will always love you, no matter what!"

Since our sons were playing at their friends' houses, Richard and I used the opportunity to go to the Minneapolis Library to see if anything had been in the newspapers. We accessed the microfilm of three newspapers from August and September of 1936 and saw six weeks of headlines about the General Hospital baby kidnapping. I read quickly.

The banner headlines described young Margaret as "immoral" and "hard boiled," a scandalous, fifteen-year-old "girl mother" and a delinquent, who had apparently conspired with Mike—who might have been my father—to murder me. My shameful roots in alcoholism, promiscuity, and attempted infanticide were laid bare in the headlines of all of the Minneapolis newspapers for nearly two months. Horrified that such a person was my birth mother, I felt ashamed of my real heritage. And, to my dismay, no matter how much I searched the newspaper coverage, nowhere did I find Mike's last name.

Reading the newspaper accounts sickened me. I was sick to my stomach as we left the library, heading home before our sons were due back. In shock, I could hardly talk. I couldn't believe that I had a mother who was a sexy materialistic delinquent who could actually send off her newborn baby to certain death. Until that day, I had spent thirty-one years thinking that I was one person—Lorene Hermanson—only to find out that I was not. I was Shirley Ann Bolin. I was not Scandinavian, not Norwegian, but Irish. I was not the daughter of disciplined, strict parents who worked hard all their lives, but the child of an immoral and promiscuous alcoholic. I was not the daughter of upstanding parents who were devoted to their deep and rich Lutheran church life, but the child of a girl who had turned her back on her Catholic background. I was not cherished by a mother who had an all-encompassing love for me, but was discarded by a mother who saw me as nothing more than a problem to be disposed of, a piece of trash.

My mother and father, Ole and Inga Hermanson, gave me a wholesome upbringing and an idyllic childhood in a large, close-knit, and church-centered family. Throughout my life, they had taught me to attend church every Sunday, and to live my life according to the proper standards of female behavior: no drinking, no smoking, and no swearing. But my birth mother had indulged in everything that I was raised to reject. She certainly lived in a different world from mine, and I shuddered to think of what would have become of me if she had raised me.

I began to wonder about her. What had happened to Margaret Bolin? Had she changed? Did she really only care about money and appearance, or had she grown into a woman with more heart and depth? I wondered, too, whether Mike was really my father. Was he also the father of the Willow River baby? Who was that poor soul? Did Mike kill that baby? How close did I come to meeting the same fate? I knew that I needed answers, needed to know the truth about my real parents. No matter what, I would learn the truth about my parents, my birth, my intended murder, and the other baby who met the fate that I had been spared.

Since the Willow River baby had died, I realized that my mother had spoken the truth: She had saved my life. In a way, this realization was devastating. I was to be drowned in Lake Calhoun or, perhaps, in the Willow River. Just as that baby had died, I would have, too, if my mother had not accidentally heard of the plot, pleaded for my life, and taken me home to pretend that I was hers. I shivered to think that I had almost died, that my life was nearly snuffed, just as it had started. I had been spared only by an accident of fate. By grace alone, my mother happened to overhear the young parents talking about their plot and she had rescued me only moments before I was to be stuffed into a black bag and thrown into a lake to drown. As awful as that felt, I also felt washed with a warmth of kinship with that other baby. She and I were somehow related, and I knew that our lives would forever be intertwined.

Thinking about that baby, I wondered if we were sisters. When I learned the real story, I felt I had the responsibility to tell the truth about Margaret, that I was her long-lost daughter and that I hadn't been drowned in Lake Calhoun but was very much alive. I would come to regret that decision but, at the time, I didn't know better, and I thought that it was the right thing to do.

From the distance of thirty-one years, the truth was hard to tell, but I felt a powerful need to know who my father was. Though the question was infused with anxiety, I needed to find out. And I needed answers to so many other questions, as well. I had some experience doing investigations in my profession and figured this background would help me conduct research into what had happened more than three decades earlier.

As a credit manager, I managed accounts for my employer, and I had a couple of years of experience in skip tracing—finding people who had skipped out and failed to pay their bills. So I decided to use my experience in skip tracing to investigate my own case, the case of the General Hospital kidnapping.

But I wondered if investigating would be dangerous, since both of my natural parents had wanted to drown me. It depended on their motives. Margaret likely just wanted to get rid of her problem, but Mike was a different story. He had money. If he were my father, he would have been afraid that I might have wanted to inherit some of his wealth when he died, or maybe I would make a paternity claim against him while he was alive. And, since he thought that the case of the kidnapped Shirley Ann was in his distant past, dead and buried, he would not welcome the bad publicity, or the truth. People like Mike will stop at nothing to keep their money and their reputations, such as they are. Of course, all I wanted was the truth, but Mike surely did not. As I realized that he might still have a reason to see me as a threat, I was filled with a real and looming fear. If I showed up alive, would Mike still want to kill me?

It scared me to the bone, just thinking that he had wanted me dead, that he had actually planned—with malice aforethought—to drown me, and that he had actually followed through in killing the Willow River baby. For all these years, my life had been a threat to him. In fact, it was possible that I was actually a greater threat now. I recognized that it could be dangerous for me to investigate, and I was very afraid that my family and I were in danger, but I needed to come to terms with my birth story, once and for all, and to find out the truth, I had to solve an old crime.

The next day, I felt strong enough to tell my sons what had had happened with my mother. The older of the two, Lonnie, was in middle school, while Ronnie was in grade school.

Though I still found it hard to believe that my entire foundation in life was not what it had always seemed to be, my sons took the news well. At least I didn't need to worry about them.

I went on with my life, performing my daily tasks as usual. But another part of my brain seemed to be watching myself living my life, going to my job as an accountant, coming home to fix dinner, and spending time with my family. It was as if I no longer existed, as if I wasn't me. I went through the motions of my life, wondering who I really was. I felt like I had a split personality, two separate parts of myself: the physical part that went about living my life, and the mental part, which was distinctly different, a new person, a woman I didn't know, a woman who was Irish and whose parents were no-good strangers.

Despite my shock, I soon developed a great sense of gratitude toward my mother, who had saved my life and raised me. She and I had always had such a special relationship. And she and my father had, without any doubt, utterly changed my life from what it would have been. And I realized that the teenagers who discarded me—Margaret and Mike—were not my real mother and father. My real mother and father were the ones who saved me, loved me, and raised me. I realized that, with some help from God, I did have the parents that I was meant to have. It takes more than giving birth to be a parent.

And though I was grateful to my mother with all my life and heart, I still did not attend her wedding when she married George. Right or wrong, I couldn't make myself go. Had she married a Christian man, I would have been delighted for her, but I am a person with convictions and I usually stick with them. When it came to my mother and her happiness and well-being, I was determined to stand for what was right. She married George in a Minnesota church and then, after the ceremony, they had a wedding dance in Wisconsin. She called me the day after the wedding and said that she missed us. It took a little while but, in the end, she admitted that I was right. The marriage was a mistake.

For the most part, I stuck to my ultimatum and never let George visit my home, but one time I let him come. I regretted it. He sneaked into our family room and found two collector bottles of whiskey that we never intended to drink, and drank them both dry. But that was nothing compared to what he proved capable of.

Later, George was accused of raping a young girl when he was drunk. He always claimed innocence and my mother believed him, but I never did. I knew that he was capable of anything when he was drunk. He spent two years in the State Prison in Waupun, Wisconsin and, eventually, my mother divorced him.

# 15

# Tнє Nuяsє in tнє Bluє Dяєss

Inga Hermanson had worked at Minneapolis General Hospital, doing housekeeping duties in the nurses' residence adjacent to the hospital. At five-foot-three inches tall, Inga had bright blue eyes and she looked neat and crisp, like all of the hospital's Scandinavian staff. On August 4th, Inga was at work, wearing her usual white uniform, when she happened to be on the third-floor maternity ward in the main hospital building, down a hallway near the back stairs. She heard two teenagers talking. A young patient stood outside her room, using hushed tones as she discussed something with her visitor, a teenage boy. Inga happened to hear them talk about getting rid of the girl's baby, and then the boy said that he would drown it in Lake Calhoun.

Hearing what they conspired to do, Inga revealed herself and walked right up to the young couple. "Please, don't do that," she pleaded. "Please, let me have her!"

Surprised to realize that their plot had been overheard, Mike was alarmed, but he welcomed the offer that would relieve him of the task of disposing of the infant. He didn't care where the baby went, as long as he was not going to be held responsible for it.

"Get it out of the hospital before five-thirty tomorrow morning," he said, "or she's gone."

"I will," Inga said. "I will."

At twenty-nine years of age, Inga had been married to Ole for four years. Though she had always hoped and assumed that she and Ole would have children soon, it hadn't happened, and Ole was forty-three years old, fourteen years older than she was. Like everyone in her family, she loved babies and children, and she had long since wanted to start a family. But, like this? If it meant saving the life of an innocent baby, she was all for it. Besides, she had heard about the teenage mother, who didn't seem to care about her beautiful, precious baby, and she realized that the baby needed her.

Inga would have considered telling the police, but at that time and place, the police were not to be trusted. Thanks to the corruption in the Twin Cities, she—and everyone—was afraid of the police and other government officials, who only looked after the interests of rich people, like the teenage boy who wanted to get rid of the baby.

Before she left her shift, Inga arranged to take a two-week vacation from her job at the hospital. Then, after work, she called her parents on the farm in Wisconsin. She told her mother and father about the conversation she'd overheard and explained that the young mother, Margaret, and her boyfriend, Mike, planned to take the baby, who was just over a week old, out of the hospital to murder her. When she talked with Ole about the situation, he was in complete agreement over the decision to save the life of the baby.

Early on the morning of August 5th, Inga got dressed, but she did not put on her usual white uniform dress. Instead, she wore a blue cotton dress with short sleeves. Carrying a large cloth tote bag that she had hand-sewn, she went to the hospital, walking through the lobby. She said good morning to the receptionist, Violet Budd, and then took the elevator to the third floor. Outside the young mother's room, Inga put a white gauze mask over her mouth. At five minutes before five o'clock in the morning, Inga, who looked like a nurse, walked into the dark hospital room and approached the bed, where the teenage mother held the infant. baby Shirley Ann wore white hospital clothes and she was wrapped in a pink receiving blanket.

Margaret handed the baby to Inga. "Here!" Margaret said. "She's all yours. I don't want her!"

At that moment, Inga became my mother.

Fully confident that she was doing the right thing—saving me from certain death at Mike's hands—my mother never doubted that God wanted her to save me. She felt no fear, but knew that she was my salvation. Since Margaret had just fed me, I was snuggled securely, swathed in a blanket and tucked into the large cloth bag. My mother left the room, walked to the elevator, and descended to the lobby, noticed by no one.

As the elevator doors opened in the lobby, Hilda Hall had just seen two teenage boys—Mike, and his bushy-haired friend—walk through the red granite lobby with a dark traveling bag.

They bounded up two flights of granite stairs to the third floor, where they planned to take the baby from Margaret. If Inga had not collected me when she did, Mike would have stuffed me in that black bag and thrown me in the lake. She had gotten me in the nick of time, with barely a moment to spare.

Lying in her bed, Margaret sighed. Sure that she would never see me again, she was glad to be rid of her baby and must have felt some measure of relief that Mike did not have to kill it. A moment later, Mike and his friend came in to Margaret's room. Margaret told him that the nurse had taken the baby away, as planned.

"Good," Mike said. "She's gone, and we don't have to drown her."

Margaret's roommate, Mrs. Maude Wolf, heard this remark. But, later, when the police interviewed her, they did not believe that she was telling the truth, so they dismissed it.

When my mother walked through the hospital lobby, Hilda Hall tended to her work at the front desk without really noticing her, since she was accustomed to seeing my mother coming and going at various shifts. No one ever questioned my mother about the missing baby, and she was never a suspect. Though Margaret claimed that a "nurse in blue" took her baby, the officials never believed her, since the hospital superintendent said that there were no nurses in blue. He and everyone else believed that outsiders took the baby, not anyone from General Hospital.

While Margaret claimed, at one point, that "Agnes Hermanson" had taken her baby, this clue never led back to my mother, probably because Margaret mixed up the name and remembered it wrong, implicating Mike's seamstress friend. Likely, when Margaret confronted Agnes Hermanson face-to-face, she realized that she was the wrong woman, but she did not know or remember my mother's name. Since Margaret had lost all credibility, her claims that a hospital employee took the baby had no weight and, therefore, my mother was never involved in the investigation. As a result, my mother was never afraid that she'd be found out.

She walked out of the hospital and across the parking lot to the far end, where my father's 1934 Oldsmobile was parked by itself. She gently set her tote bag on the floor of the car, and lifted her precious baby girl out of the bag. She tucked me in to a baby basket the color of the ocean, and she snuggled me up with blankets. Next to the basket, she had a supply of diapers and formula.

While few women knew how to drive, my mother did. By the time Margaret told the maternity nurse that a "nurse in blue" had taken her baby, my mother had long since left the Minneapolis General Hospital parking lot, presumably taking a two-week vacation. With her new baby nestled in the blue basket, my mother drove eighty miles to Clear Lake, Wisconsin, to her parents' eighty-acre farm.

Meanwhile, my father was at work as a foreman at the Minneapolis Gas Company. As soon as he could, he took a two-week vacation so that he could join us in Wisconsin. My parents were lucky enough to own one car, which my mother had driven up to the farm, so my father took the train.

Everyone in my mother's family was glad to see us, welcoming me into the family. My mother's youngest sister, Gladys, was in high school, and she loved to help take care of me. Grandma and Grandpa Reindahl and all of my mother's siblings knew where I had come from. Still, they wanted me, loved me, and doted on me for the rest of my life.

Daddy's family lived on a farm about four miles down the road from my mother's parents' place, so he traveled back and forth between his family farm and the Reindahl farm. He told his family that his wife had given birth, and though they must have wondered why they hadn't known that a baby was coming, they never questioned that I was my Ole and Inga's natural daughter. They never learned anything different.

Soon, the *Clear Lake Star* ran an announcement that "Mr. and Mrs. Ole Hermanson are the proud parents of a baby girl." Before the end of my mother's vacation, the family pastor at the Lutheran church baptized me in the rectory. My baptismal certificate would provide all the proof of birth that I would ever need.

Two weeks after we had arrived in Wisconsin, my mother and dad had to go back to Minneapolis to return to work. They left me in the good care of my mother's family, driving their Oldsmobile back to the city.

When my mother returned to work, the hospital was the center of a media storm about baby Shirley Ann. With all the intrigue and drama surrounding the "kidnapping," my mother and father were the only two people in all of Minneapolis who knew the truth. My mother went to work at the hospital, every day, carrying her secret alone. Working side by side with the nurses who had cared for the missing baby, she listened to the rumors, read the papers, heard the news on the radio, and kept a poker face. She also gave notice that she had to quit her job, saying that she was pregnant.

About two weeks later, when my mother's notice was up, she quit her job and went to Wisconsin to take care of me, spending most of the summer in Wisconsin. Everyone close to her knew the story. Finally, my father drove up to the Reindahl farm, and my parents brought me home to Minneapolis.

# 16

## I Am Your Daughter

Richard and I made several visits to the Minneapolis Library, making copies of the newspaper stories. The accounts were chilling, and I found it hard to believe that the stories were about me. I felt as though I were reading about someone else. Margaret, a liar and juvenile delinquent, was my birth mother who didn't want me. Neither did her family. By itself, that was hard to take. But it was even worse that her boyfriend had wanted to drown me and that she laughed about me being missing. When I read that Margaret had named three different fathers and that she had been drinking in beer parlors at the age of fifteen, I felt disgusted. I couldn't believe that I was the illegitimate daughter of such a girl, so young and so bad. Having been raised as a Christian woman in a strict and disciplined family, I had never even read books about wayward girls like Margaret, and I certainly never knew any such girls.

Although Alf Landon was trying to deny Franklin Roosevelt a second term as president of the United States and the Germans and Italians were interfering in the Spanish Civil War, those stories were not on the front page of the Minneapolis papers during August of 1936. That major American news was relegated to the inside pages, as Minneapolis General Hospital took up all of the page one real estate for six weeks. The story grabbed readers, with its heartache and intrigue. The public, anxious and emotional about the fate of an unloved infant, couldn't get enough information about the story of my disappearance.

When I read the coverage of the drowning of the Willow River baby, I cried. Of course, it hit home that I could have met the same fate, but it also saddened me that nobody even claimed that baby's body. If Margaret really did believe that the Willow River baby was her newborn, why didn't her family claim the baby and bury her in a cemetery plot, rather than letting the people of the town bury her in an unmarked grave? The terrible truth is that, just like Margaret, her family didn't want the baby. Though the people of Willow River symbolically adopted her and gave her a pauper's burial, she was really an orphan, unwanted, and buried like an outcast. And it was quite possibly true that she was my sister, if Mike fathered both of us. I needed to know. There were many things I needed to know.

I also felt that the right thing to do was to clear Margaret's name. For thirty-plus years, everyone who knew her believed that she had sent her baby off with Mike to certain death. Her family, friends, boyfriends, and the police all believed that she had known that Mike was going to drown the baby, and that she had handed over her baby to that fate.

Margaret had been in the Sauk Center Training School for Delinquent Girls for three years, released when she turned eighteen.

Then she served a few months of probation, living in Duluth with a minister and his wife, before she returned to Minneapolis, where she spent the rest of her life. But, three months after she returned to the city, Margaret became pregnant again. This time, she married the baby's father, Frank Albrecht.

When I learned the real story, I felt that I had the responsibility to tell the truth about Margaret—that I was her long-lost daughter and that I had not been drowned but was very much alive.

It was hard. I was so sad all the time that I was not my parents' "real" daughter. I felt bad that I didn't have a real family, like Richard did, and I carried this sadness with me. And, while I tried to act normal around my sons, they knew that I was far from all right. Though I had been unwell before my mother told me the truth, my emotional ordeal exacerbated my colitis and brought on many other illnesses. I know that, without my husband Richard, I would not have made it. He was always there to comfort and reassure me that, eventually, things would get better. But it was years before it got better.

Having conducted all the research I could at the library, I had reached the point where I was afraid of going further—afraid of being murdered, afraid for my family. And I was not alone. Richard, too, was afraid. We all were. When I took the boys to the grocery store, I could swear that someone was following me. As I walked through the aisles, I felt like someone was just around the corner, just out of eyesight. We were scared to death and looked at everyone with suspicion.

Richard felt that if we ever decided to meet Margaret, Mike, or any of the people who were involved with them, it would be safest if we did not say that we lived in Minneapolis. We decided that we would say that we lived in a Chicago suburb. To make this story seem more believable, we planned to drive a rental car and even stay in a motel, so that no one could find out where we lived. Though I felt crippled by the fear, I still wanted to move forward.

One day, I sat down with the Minneapolis telephone book. I was thinking that Margaret's mother might still be alive. I looked up her last name, Bolin, and called the first number I found. It wasn't her. I called the second number listed and a man answered. Something about his tone of voice seemed familiar to me, though I'd never spoken to anyone in that family before. Still, somehow, I knew that he was related to me.

I cleared my throat. "Yes, oh, hello," I stammered. "Is this Mrs. Bolin's home?"

"Yes," he said. "But she's in the hospital. I'm her son, John."

"Oh," I said. Thinking that the conversation was going too easily, I was surprised that he seemed so friendly. "John? Yes, well, I was trying to find Margaret, actually."

"Ah," he said. "Are you a friend, or...?"

"Hmmm," I said, vaguely.

"Well, Margaret's married," he informed me. "Her name is Albrecht now." He gave me her phone number, as well as her address, and then we said goodbye.

I trembled as I hung up the phone. Sitting there in my kitchen, I closed my eyes and bent over, crossing my arms across my belly. My gut hurt and I felt the surge of adrenaline coursing through my veins. I wanted it to stop but couldn't gain control of my feelings. All I was contemplating was dialing the phone, yet my body reacted as if someone held a gun to my temple.

I put my elbows on the table and rested my chin in my hands, closing my eyes and taking a few slow, deep breaths. "What am I doing?" I thought. "What am I doing?"

Though I was full of second thoughts, I didn't listen to them. I picked up the phone, heard a dial tone, and dialed the number that John had given me for Margaret. The phone clicked, but before it rang, I hung up. Instantly, I felt a flash of happiness, glad that I hadn't gone through with it. After all, why would I call a woman who wanted me gone or dead? I thought about my two wonderful parents and asked myself why I would want to talk with Margaret. I realized that I had many reasons for reaching out to her. I wanted to learn more about my story, wanted to know more about Margaret's family, wanted to know what kind of a woman she had become, and, more than anything, wanted to find out who my father was. If nothing else, that's all I wanted—my father.

The feeling of needing to know was intense, and it terrified me. After all, Mike was the person who was potentially capable of murder. He was the person who possibly threw a healthy infant into a river, and he was the person who had wanted me dead. Can there be any human being worse than him? Still, I wanted to know—needed to know—whether he really was my father, and Margaret was the key to that information.

I sat up straight and lifted my chest with two more deep breaths, and then I dialed the number again. Trembling, I changed my mind as the phone rang, but, this time, I didn't hang up.

"I know where your daughter is," I said in a nice telephone voice.

She hung up the phone.

Right away, I dialed her number again, but this time, the line was busy. In my frightened state, I was sure that she was calling Mike. They were still in contact with each other, and she was still trying to cover up her past. I figured that she was calling Mike, her ally in my disappearance.

I dialed again and she answered. This time, I was ready to pursue the conversation. "I am your daughter," I said.

"I thought you were dead!" she said.

"Well, no," I said. "I... My mother died recently," I lied, "and she told me about you on her deathbed." Though I am not accustomed to lying, I felt that it was necessary to protect myself and my family, especially my mother.

"Oh, my," she said, sounding friendly and interested, but a bit tentative. "Where do you live?"

"In Chicago," I lied again. "In a suburb outside of Chicago." It was hard for me to lie. As a Christian, it troubled me to say something that was untrue, but, at the same time, I could not think of any other way. I had to protect my mother and my family.

"I really thought that you were dead, and I'm so glad you're not. Are you married and all?"

I felt like she was coming on strong, as if she was being so welcoming that it was phony. Then again, I didn't know the woman, so I wouldn't know whether she was genuine or not.

"Yes," I said, speaking softly, thinking. "Yes, I'm married."

"Why don't you come out here so we can meet each other? I'd like to meet you."

I felt like she wasn't for real. "I'll talk to my husband about that and call you back," I said.

After we hung up, I felt drained. The prospect of meeting her was rife with emotion—too much emotion—and though it had been a brief phone conversation, it had filled me with distrust. I was on guard, wary of her betrayal and lies, and I realized how much work my brain had been doing throughout the few minutes we were on the phone.

I talked with Richard and decided that we would like to meet her, just once. We discussed how we needed to be very cautious, and went over our charade. We would pretend that we were flying in from Chicago, so we would rent a car, spend the night in a motel, and pretend that we knew nothing about the Twin Cities.

We were really living in Bloomington, Minnesota, a suburb of Minneapolis. We were too afraid to tell her the truth, and wanted to protect ourselves and the mother who raised me. Who, in my mind, was my *real* mother.

We set the meeting for July 27th, which, ironically, happened to be my thirty-second birthday. Margaret had not seen me since I was nine days old, and here I was, thirty-one, spending my birthday with my birth mother.

Richard and I rented a Chevrolet and drove toward her house. Part of me was in the car and another part of me was a spectator, watching over myself. It felt unreal and I felt numb, like an outsider looking in. I couldn't feel or sense anything. It was as if my senses were overloaded and the only way I could get through the ordeal was to separate myself from what I was doing, as if the union between my mind and body had been severed.

When we pulled up and parked in front of Margaret's house, it was obvious that she had been watching for us, as she came out the door and stepped off the porch, walking toward us. I was overcome. Never before had I met anyone who looked like me, and she looked exactly like me! We both had very dark brown hair and green eyes.

We were about the same height; she was about five-foot-two and I was five-foot-five. We were built the same, with small bones and size seven shoes.

But we also looked totally different from one another. If I had seen Margaret walking down the street, I would have questioned her occupation, as she wore extremely bright red lipstick and matching red polish on her fingernails and on her toenails, which showed in strappy sandals. Just as the newspapers had described her as a fifteen-year-old girl in 1936, she still wore her hair like a young girl, not a middle-aged woman. In so many ways, I could tell that she had not changed. An adult on the outside, she was a narcissistic girl on the inside, it was clear.

To me, it was horrible, a nightmare.

We said hello and introduced ourselves. Margaret said that she would have recognized me anywhere, because I looked so much like her. She also mentioned that she had been so nervous that she put on deodorant three times.

Opening the door to the backseat so that Margaret could get in the car, Richard was stunned to see someone who looked so much like me. She acted friendly enough and seemed glad to meet us, but I already knew from the newspapers that she was a good actress and a practiced liar. However, with only a fifth-grade education, she wasn't much of a conversationalist, especially on an adult level. A homemaker, she seemed to know only two subjects: housekeeping and rearing children. Conversation, therefore, was very limited. She did not know who Bach was, so it was impossible for me to discuss music with her, and Richard was a home builder and designer, which she obviously knew nothing about. As a result, the conversation was generic. While she told me that she had married the brother of her sister's husband and had eight other children, she didn't ask me about my two sons or much else.

As we drove to a restaurant, Richard and I were thinking about Mike. I was afraid that Margaret had told him about me, and Richard and I both feared that Mike would come after us. As he drove, Richard had one eye on the rearview mirror, looking to see if anyone suspicious was following us. I saw Margaret look out the rear window, and I became terribly afraid for my safety. "What in the name of God am I doing?" I thought, not at all sure that I wanted to go through with it.

"I was thinking," Margaret said. "Do you have a small brown birthmark on your left leg, below the knee?"

"I do," I said with a smile. "I have that birthmark, exactly there."

Finally, after cordial small talk, we reached the restaurant that Margaret had suggested. One of the nicer restaurants in Minneapolis, it was a supper club that was a popular nightspot.

The polite, nondescript conversation continued during dinner, with Richard and me pretending that we didn't know anything about Minneapolis. She continued to talk about her family, and she mentioned that she and her mother were meticulous housekeepers. I was also a meticulous housekeeper, but I wondered how in the world such a tendency could be inherited. Outside of looking alike, I felt that we had nothing in common.

At one point, Margaret and I got up and went to the ladies' room together. While we were alone, she said that she wondered what Richard was thinking. I could tell he made her nervous because he constantly looked at her, amazed at how much we looked alike. I assured her that it was just because we looked so much alike. In fact, in the restroom, when I looked at her, it was like looking in the mirror.

We returned to the table and talked about singers that we liked. I mentioned that I was a big fan of Engelbert Humperdinck.

"Oh, yes!" she said. "He can throw his shoes under my bed anytime!"

"He's very handsome," I nodded, thinking that too many shoes had already been thrown under her bed.

Finally, I changed the conversation. I wanted information and didn't see any reason to be less than direct.

"Who is my father?" I asked.

"I don't remember," she said nonchalantly. "I tried to remember, but I just can't. It was so long ago." Immediately, I could tell that she was lying, most likely to protect him. She was a great pretender.

"Well,'" I said, "what about Mike? The newspapers referred to the boy as 'Mike.'"

"Yes!" she said. "He's the one!"

"What's his last name?"

"Gosh, I can't remember," she claimed. "But I know that he got married and had a family."

"What nationality am I?"

"You're all Irish," she said.

Since I knew from the newspapers that Mike was Jewish, I knew that Margaret believed that he was not my father.

"Oh," she added. "Mike is also very wealthy. He owns many businesses."

I wondered how she knew this if she didn't remember his last name. She seemed just like the girl I had read about in the newspapers, manipulative and coy, hesitant to offer the truth and unwilling to just be honest. Like a child, she still seemed to be protecting the fantasy of the past.

"By the way," Margaret said. "My husband, Frank, works as a guard at the Hennepin County Jail and he doesn't even know that you exist."

"All right," I said.

Driving back to her house, I wanted to ask her why she didn't love me when I was a baby, but I knew better. She was too young when she had me, and she knew nothing about babies then. All she cared about was herself. A terrific actress, she seemed to be pretending to be someone that I knew she wasn't. Since she wouldn't tell me about my father, I felt disgusted by her selfishness. I was completely turned off by her fake friendliness and, at times, I saw a coldness in her that was disconcerting. During the drive, I couldn't even turn around and look at her in the car, thinking about the harm she had wanted to do to me as an infant.

Still, she went on and on about her other children, telling us how wonderful they were. She even told me that her favorite child was Jennifer, though we would find out later that Margaret had Jennifer while Frank was away in the military.

I was grateful that the ride to her house was quick. I felt ill and needed to get away from her. Though I was desperate for the truth, I realized that I was not going to get it. If she had told me, it would have made such a difference, but she had no interest in helping me. Just like the younger version of Margaret that I'd read about in the newspapers, she was still a psychopathic, narcissistic liar. All she cared about were money and appearances.

When we parked in front of Margaret's house, she suggested that we see her again the next day and visit her mother in the hospital. Barbara Bolin had suffered complications from diabetes, and Margaret thought that I might like to meet my grandmother. After meeting Margaret, I wasn't at all sure that I wanted to meet her mother, so I don't know why, but I agreed to go with her to the hospital the next day.

That night, I did not sleep at all. My only comfort was in praying, and I found myself constantly asking God for protection from evil and forgiveness for my own deceits. I was still wide awake when the sun came up, so the next day, I was exhausted and felt ill. I was also very concerned about meeting Margaret's mother. I knew that, in 1936, she had told the police that she didn't want Margaret to bring me home. I approached that afternoon with dread.

Again, we drove to Margaret's house to pick her up. To my relief, she was more relaxed and much friendlier. She greeted me by saying that I looked pretty, so we were off to a good start that day. Then, when I met Barbara, it was love at first sight. The grand dame of the family, she loved to entertain over a cup of tea. When we walked into her hospital room, she looked to be in her sixties, with greying hair. She was being discharged from the hospital in a few days and was looking well, though half of her left leg had been amputated below the knee due to her diabetes. She stretched out her arms to me and started crying.

A typical Irish woman with "the gift of the gab," she said that she wished that my grandfather had been there so that he could see me. Bert had passed away about eight years earlier, so I never met him. Tall and slim, he had been a sheet-metal worker and everyone spoke very highly of him.

While we visited, Grandmother Bolin did most of the talking. She told us how glad she was to meet us and how much she loved me, and, other than that sort of thing, it was mostly small talk, but I laughed and smiled and cried the whole while I was with her. We stayed with her for about an hour and, when it was time to go, she didn't want us to leave. I felt as if she feared that she would never see me again and, as we wrapped up the visit, she began planning our next visit. She wanted to have a picnic for us the next time we came. Richard and I felt good around her, and I assured her that we would meet again.

Before long, Grandmother Bolin and I had a special bond, and we loved each other very much. In many ways, she made my pain bearable. And, though I knew that I would never call Margaret "mother," I had no problem calling my grandmother "Grandmother."

Of course, the mother who had raised me was a wonderful mother and I loved her with all of my heart, and I wasn't sure if I even liked Margaret. In the end, I realized that I shouldn't have allowed Margaret into my life at all. I would have been better off if I had never met her. We drove back to Margaret's house and dropped her off, and then we drove back to the car rental agency and returned the car. We felt overwhelmed. Driving home, we thought about all that had happened in the last twenty-four hours. We were clear that we liked my grandmother, but our feelings about Margaret were very confused. She seemed unhappy and phony, and I have never liked people like that.

After what she had done to me, I thought that the least she could do was to tell me the truth about my father, but she couldn't even do that. Didn't she know that I needed to know the whole truth about

1936, that I was desperate to know whether my father was Mike or Larry O'Reilly or some other man? After all, I was an adult. After so many years, didn't Margaret want to unburden herself by telling the truth? After more than thirty years, why couldn't she let it go? Why wouldn't she?

As we drove home, Richard nervously checked the rear view mirror all the way. We were exhausted and talked about Margaret and Barbara as if we were debriefing each other after all of the conversations we'd had during the previous day. The more we talked, the less we liked Margaret. And my sense of distrust—of both Margaret and Mike—did not dissipate. If anything, it grew.

As part of our scheme of pretending we lived in Chicago, we promoted the pretense that we were heading to the airport to fly home. Since Margaret had asked us to call her before we boarded our plane, I called her from home, acting as if we were waiting for our flight. I was dismayed at that conversation.

Margaret told me that her husband Frank was sick and that she needed to pay his life insurance, in case he died. She told me that she didn't have the money and she needed more than one hundred dollars to pay the premium. Trying to sound concerned for her husband, she poured on the charm in a phony-sweet tone of voice. While she tried to talk me into giving her what she wanted, she reminded me of the manipulative girl that I had read about in the 1936 newspapers.

I was shocked. "I don't have that much cash with me," I said.

As she replied, I thought of her as an actress who was playing a part. "Oh, of course," she said sweetly. "Even if you could send me fifty dollars when you get home, that would help," she added, pouring on the charm as she played the role of a worried, down-and-out wife.

154

Of course, I knew that she was lying. Margaret's husband Frank was a very healthy man who worked for Hennepin County, which paid for all of his benefits, including insurance.

At the end of the call, Margaret said that we were wonderful and she wished that she could go home with us. Of course, coming from a liar, it didn't mean much to me. As we hung up, Margaret suggested that I should call her sometime and I said I would, though I wasn't too sure about that.

After I hung up, I felt so disappointed. After reading all the newspaper accounts about Margaret and her attitude, I wasn't exactly surprised to find that she had not changed in thirty years, but I guess I had hoped that she had grown up some in that time. I had hoped that she would have told me the truth. But some things never change and Margaret obviously had not. She was exactly the same person she was when she was fifteen: a greedy liar.

I wished that my mother had never told me the truth. I was a good person—a giver, not a taker—and I did not deserve to be in this situation, with a mother who was so selfish and materialistic, manipulative and dishonest. I started to cry.

I never sent any money to Margaret, but I did send her a dozen red roses. We ordered them from a florist and included a small card. I figured that, through the years, Margaret had probably never received roses from anyone and, if I never saw her again, she would remember the roses and think about me once in a while.

# 17

## SHAME

When I turned up and injected myself into Margaret's life, my existence confronted her with the undeniable truth: Thirty-one years after she'd identified the dead Willow River baby as her missing infant, her first-born child actually was alive. Any woman who has held her newborn baby in her arms knows that it is hard to imagine any woman mistaking another baby for her own—especially after having held and nursed that baby for nine days. But that Margaret made such a mistake in identifying the dead baby as her own is simply testament to the distance with which she regarded her own first child. As everyone knew, the fifteen-year-old Margaret cared more about her lipstick than she did her baby, so it is reasonable to conclude that she simply did not discern the differences between her baby and the Willow River baby.

The nurses, however, who doted on baby Shirley Ann, noticed the differences between the missing baby and the found one, and as a result, the only evidence linking Margaret with the murdered150infant was her own identification of her. Had she claimed that the deceased infant was not her child, the investigators would have believed her without much doubt, despite her reputation for producing automatic lies. But Margaret panicked. With little recall of the details of baby Shirley Ann's appearance, which lacked the marks of forceps and but included adhesive from the sticker on her back, Margaret knew only that she and Mike had planned to drown the baby, so she assumed that the drowned infant was hers.

In a sense, she hanged herself. If Margaret had taken a few good, long looks at her own baby while she was cradled in her arms, the young mother would have known that hers was not the infant lying on a crate in the funeral home, and she would not have provided the evidence tying her predicament with that horrible outcome. But, because she lied, she suffered the consequences, spending nearly three years in the Sauk Center detention home. After all, she left the officials no alternative when she provided the proof that her baby was dead.

I imagined what it must have been like for Margaret at fifteen, eighteen, thirty, and forty—all her adult life—for everyone who knew her to have believed that she had planned to have her own newborn killed. I wondered what Barbara Bolin must have thought about her oldest daughter's heartless values, and the example that she set for her younger sisters and brothers. I wondered what her boyfriends and other men in her life thought of a beautiful young woman who could do such a thing. I wondered what kinds of scandalous whispers and looks she got from her neighbors and from strangers who learned that she was the girl mother about whom they had read in the newspapers.

Had she felt the shame? Had she been ostracized? How much had it cost her?

Thirty-one years later, I felt that I needed to do my part in vindicating Margaret. It seemed to me that I had the responsibility to clear her name, to come forward and show everyone—especially her relatives—that Margaret's baby was not dead, and that Margaret, therefore, had not killed her own child, even though she and Mike had discussed doing so and even though Mike had possibly been responsible for killing another newborn, the Willow River baby. Though I felt no tug at my heartstrings and no interest in having a relationship with my birth mother, I felt that showing myself was the right thing to do. Not that she did, but if my birth mother deserved anything from me, she deserved that truth.

That was why I reached out to her, even though I didn't have to and even though it was very difficult for me emotionally, physically, and financially. Of course, I wanted something in return, which Margaret never gave me. But she also never gave me any credit for vindicating her. I might have felt differently about her if she had acknowledged the difficulty that the situation caused for me but, as she later proved, she cared little about me or my ordeal, so I soon regretted reaching out to her, meeting her, and even vindicating her.

I wanted to remain a faithful daughter to my real mother—the one who saved my life, the one who raised me. More important than anything, I did not want to hurt Mother, so I never wanted her to know that I had met Margaret. She was a wonderful Christian woman, a loving mother to me and a generous grandmother to my sons, and after she told me how she had saved my life, we never discussed it again.

Days followed days in which I tried to adjust to the shock of finding out about my birth mother. I also tried—unsuccessfully—to ignore my heritage in the Bolin family. I felt extremely ashamed of Margaret: with her crudeness and her lifestyle of drinking, smoking, and swearing. Unaccustomed to such behavior, I felt horrified that I was actually related to such people and that I was the daughter of such a selfish, vain woman. Worse, it bothered me that Margaret had been a juvenile delinquent, twice sentenced to the Sauk Center Training School for Delinquent Girls. And I felt deeply ashamed that I had been an illegitimate baby, with an unknown father, and that I had been given away because I was unwanted. I couldn't bring myself to tell my friends or my in-laws that my birth mother had planned to kill me, to throw me away like trash. I couldn't get over it, and I suffered a great deal as my mother's secret became my secret.

I carried the truth about myself as I went about living my life, dedicated to my job and generous with my time as a volunteer. Unlike Margaret and her family, I came from a family of good, wholesome folks who would give anyone the shirts off their backs. I was a Bible camp counselor, Sunday School teacher, and fund raiser for school and church. An Irish tenor, I was a church organist and soloist, and I sang for weddings, funerals, and other services, and I gave free voice lessons to little girls who wanted to become church singers. Thank God for the loves of my life—music and my husband Richard; they helped me to overcome my pain and kept me sane. While I felt as if I were a lesser person because I had been a white-trash, throwaway baby, my music reminded me that, in the eyes of Jesus, I was as good as anyone else.

There's an old saying that "Music doth calm the savage beast." In my case, that was literally true.

As I investigated the past and tried to assimilate the awful truth into my perception of myself, I also fought it. I didn't want it to be real, didn't want to be Margaret's daughter in any way, so Richard and I kept it between us. At the same time, I needed to come to terms with it, and that meant that I had to learn the whole story, so I obsessed with the need to know about my father. Full of conflict, I fought a constant battle inside myself.

I also felt threatened, almost constantly. My living room had a large picture window with a view of the street, and I had a sheer curtain so I could see out but no one could see inside. Two weeks after I met Margaret, I noticed a car parked in front of our house when Richard wasn't home. A man sat behind the steering wheel of the large, brand-new black sedan. Richard was working on a home nearby and usually came home at noon to check on me. As soon as he pulled his car into the driveway, the black car drove away. But after Richard left again, the car returned. Since the car sat outside every day, Monday through Friday, week in and week out, for more than two months, I felt like a prisoner in my own home.

I wrote down the car's license plate number and tried to track down the driver, but I found out that the car belonged to a rental company that refused to give me any information. Still, I was sure that the car was connected to Mike or his brother, Al. The two of them had plenty of connections and they could do anything; finding out where I lived would have been easy for them. And even though Margaret played along with our story about living in the Chicago area, I was also convinced that she knew where we lived.

Every morning, I drove my sons to school and then returned home, driving quickly into the garage and closing the door with the automatic garage-door opener. Frightened when I was home alone, I wouldn't open the front door for anyone without looking through the peep-hole in the door, or I would look out the window to see if I recognized a car. I tried not to go out alone, but to be with Richard or my sons whenever I left the house. And when I took the freeway, I usually drove very fast so that anyone who was following me would have been obvious. I was a nervous wreck, and the stress was getting to me.

Before I met Margaret, I had some minor health problems, but after my mother told me the true story of my birth, and then after meeting Margaret, I became very ill. I needed two surgeries, I had an ulcer and ulcerative colitis, which was severe. Colitis is incurable. While patients can control it with medical help, the disease can flare up at any time and, when doctors cannot stop the bleeding and get the wounds to heal, bad flare ups can be fatal. Before long, my colitis was greatly exacerbated by my feelings about Margaret. The stress of my emotional turmoil was destroying my health.

I consulted with the best gastroenterologist around. "What's eating at you?" he asked. "We need to solve the problem." But I was so mortified about my emotional issues—shame, anger, sadness—that I knew I would burst into tears and cause a big scene if I were to try to explain. I couldn't bring myself to tell him. Other doctors told me the same thing, that something was "eating away" at me and that I needed to solve my emotional issues. They offered to help, if I would let them, but I just could not bring myself to talk to them about my family history. It was too much. It felt too big.

Besides, I had a good sense of what would help me: I wanted to know about my father. And after what I had done for Margaret, I thought that the least she could do was to tell me the truth about my father and his identity. That was the only thing I wanted from her.

I also wanted to know the whole truth about my story. I felt as though my whole life was a lie. In a way, I did not know who I was. I doubted my upbringing, my past, my wholesome, idyllic childhood. I wondered if I really was the Irish daughter of a "sport" or the morally upstanding daughter of two of the most decent people I had ever known. I was desperate to know the whole story, all of it, and I felt that I had the right to know.

Throughout my life, I had worked hard to be the very best that I could be at my jobs, music, and everything that I tried to do. I had grown accustomed to having this sort of control over my own life, but suddenly, I had lost that sense of control. In terms of my very essence— my existence—suddenly had no control. All I had was a birth mother who wanted me dead. Like most adopted children who want to know about their heritage, I had a passion to find out. And I thought that learning the truth might improve my health in the process.

I was very upset that Margaret and Grandmother Bolin refused to tell me who my father was. Margaret had had thirty years to get the courage to tell the truth, but she never did reveal it. It's perplexing that she would rather have people think she killed her own baby than to simply reveal the truth about who had fathered the child. In any case, she still wasn't talking, and all I had to go on was that they had said that I was one-hundred-percent Irish. Although I didn't know anything about Mike—not even his last name—I knew from the newspapers that Larry O'Reilly was Irish. Maybe he was my father.

Still, we were afraid of Mike. According to the public record, no one knew who the father really was.

When Margaret had asked me for money after our first visit, I felt utterly disgusted. I did not want to see her ever again. But I doubted that I could learn about my father without her.

# 18

# GRANDMOTHER BOLIN

While I didn't like Margaret, I liked her mother very much. Outgoing, vivacious, and funny, she had a vibrant, sincere personality and she was welcoming and open with me. If I had any hope of learning about my father, I invested it in Barbara, figuring that she was the only person who would help me. That motivation moved me to keep in touch with her, but it was my fondness for her that helped me to build a special relationship with my long-lost grandmother.

One day, when I was physically and emotionally up to it, I decided to call Grandmother Bolin. When she answered the phone and I told her it was me, I heard her sniffle.

"I'm so glad to hear from you!" she cried. "I missed you! I was wondering when you were going to call..."

She was the kind of person who expressed what was on her mind and in her heart. Unlike her eldest daughter, Grandmother Bolin was emotionally honest, not afraid to be herself and to put herself out there. She was fun to be around, but from what I had learned from my uncle, she had been a bit wild in her younger days, partying and drinking. By the time I met her, she'd had one leg amputated, and that had slowed her down. I'm glad that I didn't meet her when she was into her partying lifestyle, though Grandmother Bolin and her friends told me many stories about her younger days, when she knew how to have a good time. Grandmother was incredibly funny and fun to be around, in spite of some crudeness that usually made me cringe.

Of everyone in the family, Grandmother was most welcoming, and when I talked to her, she wanted to see me. Still believing that I lived in Chicago, she asked when I would be able to come back to Minneapolis, and she expressed that she hoped I would be able to visit soon. She specifically asked me to come to her house so that she and I could talk one-on-one. I said I would try to come soon.

Despite the fact that she was getting on in years and significantly suffering from the complications of her diabetes, Grandmother still managed to have fun, and her delightful gift of gab persisted through-out her life. I enjoyed our frequent talks as I learned a lot about her, and we developed a wonderful relationship. After Margaret, Grand-mother had raised six children—Barbara, Rosie, Nanny, Betty, Del-bert, and John—so her life had been full and busy.

Soon after our first visit with Margaret and Grandmother, Rich-ard and I pretended to fly in from Chicago again. We went to my grandmother's house for a visit, and we met one of Margaret's sisters, my Aunt Betty. Betty and I hit it off instantly and Richard also hit it off with Betty's husband, Earl Kommerstad. We looked forward to spending more time with them.

That summer, when we visited with the Bolins again, I met Margaret's brothers, Delbert and John. Two years older than I was, Delbert was the Bolin son whom the police had thought was actually Margaret's child, not Barbara's. Whether he was my uncle or my brother, the question really wasn't a legal issue, though it had been a part of the investigation into Margaret's background and her character. As far as I knew, the police had not pursued it, but since Delbert had been born at home, his birth certificate may or may not have been accurate. Besides, as far as I know, no one ever saw Delbert's birth certificate. So, whether he was Margaret's brother or mine, I don't know, but he looks exactly like Margaret. A soft-spoken man, he was always very nice to me.

Richard and I also met John that summer. John, who was in his thirties, felt sorry for me and tried to be my friend, treating me better than any of the rest of them ever did. I liked him very much, partly because he told Richard about all of the family's dirty laundry. I think that, if he had known who my father was, he would have told me. In the summer of 1969, as Grandmother Bolin's health was failing, John moved into the house next door to her so that he could be involved in her care. He was devoted to his mother. A gifted athlete, John had been the top-ranked basketball player in the state, earning a college scholarship but, rather than attend college, he had gone to work to support his mother. In her later years, he cared for her every day after work.

Another of Margaret's sisters was Rosie, whom I liked. She cared for Grandmother Bolin during the day. Grandmother was on disability and county assistance, and Rosie got paid by the county to help her mother. Rosie was married to Richard Albrecht, the brother of

Margaret's husband, Frank. Like Frank, Dick was an alcoholic. When everyone thought that we were living in Chicago, we had to fly there from Minneapolis to meet Margaret's sister and her husband. The lie had gotten to be too much.

I didn't want to have anything more to do with Margaret, but then her sister Helen called Grandmother and told her that her husband's company was sending them to Chicago and, while she was there, she wanted to meet me.

I was sick of living a lie and afraid not to, so we also had to fly to Chicago, since that's where we pretended to live. We rented a car, met Helen and her husband Donald at their hotel, and went out to dinner with them, and I found them extremely nice. We had some good conversations. Donald was a nice man, as was their son, Timothy, who was in junior high school.

I found myself wishing that Margaret was more like her sister Helen. Though the women did have one bad trait in common, the only thing that bothered me about Helen. She seemed to be money-driven. Her husband had a very good-paying job, and Helen was the wealthiest of Margaret's siblings. Wearing a diamond ring on every finger, she tended to emphasize material possessions and focus on how much money people had.

The situation left me terribly stressed and I wondered when it would end. I couldn't sleep or eat. Even though I liked all of my new aunts and uncles, and loved my grandmother, I knew that it was a big mistake to get involved with Margaret's family. Plus, Mike was looming over us. I had gone this far and still needed to know who my father was to finish the puzzle. I just couldn't get over that. All I needed was to know Mike's last name. Then again, I recalled the1936 reports, in which my grandmother had told the police that a boy named Larry O'Reilly was my father.

Richard and I didn't want to pretend anymore, especially since my grandmother was getting quite frail and wanted me to come and see her more often. So in 1974, we told them that we were moving to the Twin Cities. That made things much easier. After that, I started to feel real connection with some of my aunts and uncles, especially with Grandmother Bolin.

She and I developed a real bond, and I enjoyed a close relationship with her. She always wanted me to come over and see her, which I did, visiting her weekly. Margaret's children became jealous of this special bond. I would meet some of her Irish friends, who were just like her, and Grandmother Bolin told everyone that I was "sweetest girl that ever lived." Despite the fact that she had not wanted her fifteen-year-old daughter to bring me home as a newborn baby, I felt like my grandmother was making up for that and for the thirty-plus years when I knew nothing about Margaret's family. She seemed to be very emotional about welcoming me into the family, and I got the impression that it was important to her to show me attention and affection. I appreciated it. It seemed as though that wonderful upbringing that I had was new to all of Margaret's relatives. Grandmother Bolin cried every time I left her house. When one of my cousins became engaged to be married, Grandmother planned the wedding. She asked me to play the organ for the wedding and to sing the beautiful song "Amazing Grace." I even did the altar flower arrangement, which was something I was good at. The day of the wedding, my grandmother was in a wheelchair and my Uncle John wheeled her right up to the front of the church, as close to the organ as he could get her.

One of Margaret's sisters was sitting in front of Margaret, and when I sang "Amazing Grace," she turned to look at Margaret. Tears were rolling down Margaret's cheeks. The words must have tugged at her heartstrings a little, especially the words "I once was lost but now am found."

I also became good friends with Margaret's sister, Betty. With our husbands, we would do things together as a foursome—going out to dinner and a show, having each other over for dinner and then playing cards, or going out to concerts and such. One time, we went to an Englebert Humperdinck concert together. For a while, we were truly good friends, and she told me some of the inside story about Margaret. For example, she confided in me that the paternity of some of Margaret's children was questionable. In an effort to help me, she also once confronted Margaret in a very tough, aggressive tone, trying to get her sister to divulge Mike's last name. Even that was futile. Margaret would not tell the truth, no matter what.

Strangely, Margaret called me at home a lot of times, late at night, when she was drunk. She would call around ten o'clock at night and ramble on about nothing. Of course, I tried to take advantage of these conversations but I soon learned that it didn't matter how drunk she was, she still wouldn't give me Mike's last name or my father's identity. So, when she was drunk, I did not talk to her. Usually, I just got rid of her.

But, one night when she called, I told her about something silly that I had done. I sang with Sweet Adelines and we were having "Crazy Quartet Week," a fun break from our regular rigorous practice schedule. One of the members of our quartet played a woman who was nine months pregnant, while the rest of us played her suitors. I played

Groucho Marx, another woman wore a Boy Scout uniform, and the last dressed up as a sailor as we sang "Who's Sorry Now." Evidently, from the vantage point of a middle-aged woman with a complex background, Margaret did not think that the specter of a pregnant girl with three suitors was funny. "Shammy, little girl," she said, as if she was scolding a young child. "Mustn't do that!"

To me, it was nothing but strange that my birth mother would scold me as if I were one of her little children for portraying a woman like the girl she had been in a farce.

I wondered if she tended to call when she was drunk because the alcohol helped her feel uninhibited: less cold, and more in touch with whatever maternal feelings she might have had for me. I doubted that she had any such feelings, though I had seen glimpses of something that indicated such instincts, in the accounts of her reaction to seeing the dead Willow River baby, for example. Still, a part of me wondered if, maybe, she missed me—and maybe she needed the drink to get up her courage to call and talk to me. Since she just rambled about inconsequential things, I had no way of knowing why she really called or what she might have felt when she did so.

One day in the midmorning, when Margaret's children would have been in school, I decided to go to her house to try to talk with her. I still wanted her to tell me the truth about 1936, about my father, about all that had happened, and I figured that, maybe, if I confronted her in person without warning, I could catch her off-guard and impress upon her my need to know. I showed up at her house at ten in the morning, determined to get Mike's last name, at least.

Margaret met me at the front-porch door. She was drunk. She told me that she had been ironing all morning and wanted only to say hi, since she had not known that I was coming. Acting coldly, she did not welcome my visit and, in fact, would not let me into her house.

I pleaded with her, telling her that I was really suffering, not knowing who my real father was.

She lit into me. "No one has suffered like I have," she barked at me. "I'm the only one that suffered! You never suffered!" Then she retreated into her porch and slammed the door in my face.

Stunned, I went home. It was quite a while before I contacted Margaret again, as my health declined with each encounter.

By the spring of 1974, under a doctor's care, my health improved. Physically better and stronger, I planned a trip to Ireland with Richard and some friends. In order to travel out of the country, I needed to get a passport, and that process required that I get my birth certificate. I had never had one. Throughout my life, my mother had used my baptismal certificate as my proof of birth. When I went to the county records office and found my original birth certificate, it said "Baby Girl Bolin, illegitimate."

The word "illegitimate" should never be printed on anyone's birth certificate. It's degrading. I felt ashamed when I had to use this birth certificate to obtain my passport. Later, I had my name added to it: Lorene Joyce Bolin. I had to sign and swear to it, under oath.

In Ireland with friends, we went to Galway, which is where Grandmother Barbara McDonough Bolin had come from. Almost all of the women my age looked just like me and I passed for a native. We found that many businesses in Galway had the McDonough name on them, and all of the McDonoughs we met were extremely friendly and welcoming. They knew by looking at me that I was one of them. All I needed was the Irish brogue, but I felt at home there, as if I belonged.

I hated to leave Ireland. This was 1976. We were living in Mendota Heights, Minnesota.

Back at home, I also learned that Grandmother Bolin was a first cousin to John McDonough, the longest-seated mayor of St. Paul, Minnesota. The city has a John McDonough Day, and has named parks and housing projects after him. Prominent in St. Paul politics, that part of the family was not close to the Minneapolis McDonoughs.

Still feeling well, I decided to call Margaret on the phone one day. "I thought you died!" she said.

What a nice greeting, I thought, though the conversation improved as Margaret sounded warm and friendly. I was glad to hear her like that, so I was a little more receptive to her than I normally was. She wanted us to come to her house the next day. My first reaction was that I did not want to go, but Margaret was very kind and persuasive. I had not seen her or her siblings in quite a while, so I opened up to the idea and finally agreed to go. I still didn't want to go, but couldn't think of a reason to turn down the invitation, so I said that we would come. I am not sure why I agreed to it, but I did.

That night, anticipating the visit the next day, I didn't sleep a wink. In my gut, I felt sheer dread of seeing her again and knew that I'd made a mistake in agreeing to go. I realized that her sweet and warm tone of voice on the phone had been her way of manipulating me; she had poured on the charm only because she wanted me to come. A master manipulator, she had gotten what he wanted.

Richard and I tentatively strolled up Margaret's front walk and then she emerged to guide us into her front porch, where one of her daughters was ironing. Shocked when she brought us inside her home, I really did not want to meet any of Margaret's children and I was very uncomfortable when Margaret introduced me as her friend's daughter. I realized that, before we had arrived, Margaret had told her husband and children that I was coming over, but that I was the daughter of an old friend of hers. I remembered that Margaret had previously told me that her husband did not know about me, though I knew that everyone in her family was aware that she'd had a colorful past. I smiled, though I felt sick to my stomach.

For her part, Margaret seemed more warm and friendly than she had at other times, though we only exchanged small talk, as usual. Though I could tell that she was obviously trying to be cordial and friendly—on her best behavior—none of this made me feel any better about her.

Before long, we went out to dinner. As was our routine, Richard and I drove a rented car and, as he drove, Richard kept an eye on the rear view mirror. Richard and I both still felt afraid of Mike. It was like a fear of the unknown, a fear of all the lies and the unknown motives behind them, and a fear of his money and greed.

Margaret talked a little bit about her family, and Richard and I shared some news about our two sons. Lonnie and Ronnie were good athletes involved in several sports, so we told her about that. And, as usual, I again asked her if she had remembered my father's name. She claimed that she still could not remember his name or anything else, so I didn't bother to ask her again that night.

I asked about Margaret's mother and Margaret told us that one of her sisters, Nanny, was going through a divorce was staying with her mother with her large family. Somehow, I sensed that Margaret was ashamed of this sister and all of her children, and I found out later that Nanny was very poor, which was likely the reason why. I believe that Margaret felt superior to Nanny. Margaret made it clear that it would be a bad time to visit Grandmother, so this time we didn't.

After we finished dining, Margaret said that her oldest son, Bob, frequented a certain nightclub and she suggested that we go there to see a show and maybe meet him. I still did not look forward to meeting any of her other children, but I knew that she would probably introduce me as a friend, so we agreed and went to the club. Bob didn't show up.

After a while, we suggested that it was time to go. When we took her home, she said that she hoped we would keep in touch and visit her again when we could. I wondered why she would want to have us visit. At least she hadn't asked me for money again.

After this visit, I again became very ill.

The next time we decided to visit, I mostly wanted to see my grandmother. We went straight to Grandmother Bolin's house. Two of my aunts and their husbands were there, as well as John and his fiancé. It was a hot, humid afternoon and we spent the hours visiting. It was wonderful. It was a special mix of people and I felt as though we had known each other all of our lives. The visit was infused with a real sense of belonging and, during that day, I began to develop the feeling that these people were actually becoming my other family.

In the evening, it was still quite warm when Margaret and her youngest daughter joined the party at my grandmother's house and, in a bit, Margaret's husband Frank arrived. We sat around my grandmother's table, talking and laughing.

One of my aunts wanted to have a picnic for us, but Margaret quickly told her that her oldest daughter, Patty, was having a picnic and that she would call her to ask if it was okay for the rest of us to attend the picnic. Patty said that it would be fine.

The prospect of meeting Margaret's other children at a big picnic sent me into a panic, and I literally became ill as I thought about it. "I don't think it's a good idea," I said.

"'Oh, come on," she persisted. "It'll be just great! Then everyone will have the chance to meet you, and we can keep visiting. You've got to come!"

"But we've been here all day," Richard chimed in. "We've got so much to do and..."

"Nah," Margaret insisted. "Just a few hours in the afternoon. It'll be great."

Richard checked the expression on my face as Margaret and my aunts discussed additional plans for the picnic.

Margaret left the room for a moment and her husband Frank turned to me.

"That's too bad, what happened to Margaret," he said, "or I'd be your daddy now." Frank smiled and took a quick pull from his beer.

Smiling, I didn't say anything in reply. Frank seemed like a nice enough man, but I was shocked that he would say that to me. I didn't know that he knew that I was Margaret's daughter, for one thing. Also, like Margaret, Frank was a drinker, an alcoholic. I wondered whether it was the alcohol that had caused him to be so open, though, in a way, I was grateful for his acceptance, drunk or not.

Margaret returned to the table and, a bit later, suggested that Richard and I go a short distance over to her house, because she had air-conditioning and she thought that we would be more comfortable in her cool house. I wondered who would be home. I was hesitant. From the beginning, I had felt that I had no reason in the world to want to meet Margaret's children. I already had a family—a very good, moral one—and there was no part of me that wanted to be a part of Margaret's family. I was not at all sure that I wanted to go to her house, where I felt like I did not belong. Still, I'd been enjoying the day with my grandmother, aunts and uncle, and air-conditioning sounded like a good idea. So, with my silent reservations, we went to Margaret's.

Margaret and Frank got there before we did. When we walked into her house, Margaret left the room to go get us something cold to drink.

Frank, who was sitting on the couch, looked up at me. "You look a lot like my daughter, Jennifer," he observed.

Again, I gave him a smile and acknowledged him with a noncommittal sigh. I had heard that Jennifer was possibly not his daughter, since she was born at a time when Frank was away in the military. I looked around the room. I had thought that I would never enter Margaret's house, much less be sitting there visiting with her husband while Margaret served me a drink.

When we arrived at the picnic the next day, I felt sick. I felt worse when one of my aunts told me that Margaret had said that she was going to tell her children who I was. Soon, though, I could tell that she had not told them, and I was so grateful that she hadn't. I did not want her to tell them—and she never did. Still, they found out. At the picnic, I didn't eat. My aunts could tell by looking at me that I was very upset and stressed, and they spent the party talking with me and helping me survive the hours. I felt sick the entire time I was there. It was the longest day of my life.

By the time we left the picnic, Richard and I were mentally drained.

The next day, we went over to my grandmother's house for a quick visit to say goodbye. One of my aunts was there. She told us that, after the picnic, Margaret's oldest daughter had said that she knew who I was. Sometime before that, she had applied for a passport and had to produce her birth certificate, which listed her as the second-born child of Margaret Elizabeth Bolin.

We said our goodbyes and left. Driving through Minneapolis, Richard watched his rear view mirror, exhausted. I went to bed for two weeks.

As I thought about the visit and all the people I had met, I realized what had been going on. I was Margaret's vindication. All she wanted from me was my visibility, so that she could vindicate herself. That's why she paraded me around to her relatives—her mother, sisters and brothers, and even her children. She wanted to show them that she and Mike had not killed me. It was her way of saying, "See? I didn't kill my baby!"

But the truth is that killing me is precisely what she and Mike had planned to do. If not for my mother's intervention, they would have killed me, and Margaret would not have been vindicated. The truth is that I am lucky to be alive, not because of Margaret and Mike, but in spite of them. They wanted me dead. And Margaret, who was such a dispassionate and disconnected mother that she couldn't tell the difference between her own baby and the Willow River baby, had apparently believed I was dead. At that moment, she must have assumed that something had fallen through with the "nurse in blue," that the woman had given me back to Mike, and that he had drowned me. Then again, maybe Margaret knew the dead baby wasn't her own.

Maybe she had lied, thinking that doing so would make all the fuss go away and everyone would stop asking her what happened to her baby. Maybe she never dreamed that she would be implicated in the baby's murder, since she was an invalid in the hospital at the time. Either way, before I was even born, she was complicit in a plot to do away with me, so it was really a hollow vindication that I was still alive. Were it not for my mother—Inga Hermanson—I would be dead, as dead as the Willow River baby. And it would have been Margaret's fault as much as Mike's.

I wished I hadn't allowed Margaret to parade me around. I wished that everyone in Margaret's family knew the truth, but first, I had to find out what that was.

# 19

## MIKE

Back in 1936, as the police investigation into my disappearance was gearing up, my grandmother had told the police that Larry O'Reilly was my father. Given my reading of the police reports and newspaper accounts, he seemed to be the first man whom Margaret had named as the father, and she later said that she "liked him best."

In 1976 I located Larry O'Reilly's family and was able to call his younger brother on the telephone. For a month, I had many phone conversations with him, and we became phone friends.

I always wanted to get together with him, but I had several illnesses to deal with at the time and did not manage to visit him. Much younger than Larry, he did not know about Margaret, but he didn't doubt that I might have been Larry's child.

In time, I managed to visit Larry's father. He and Larry's son lived in the house where Larry had been raised. I told him that I was helping my mother to plan a class reunion and I wondered if he would mind telling me about Larry.

A marathon runner and wonderful ballroom dancer, Larry had been married, though unhappily. Like so many American boys and men at that time, Larry had enlisted in 1941. He had joined the Army and became a paratrooper in World War II, and his whole squadron had been killed in Normandy in 1944. Larry was buried in France.

As he talked about Larry, his father showed me some pictures. When he showed me Larry's graduation picture, I could see right off that I looked just like him. We had the same coloring—green eyes and brown hair. He told me that Larry's marriage had been a very unhappy one, and showed me Larry's wedding picture, in which the bride had been cut away. He also showed me a picture of Larry's son and I was shocked. He was a twin for my son, Lonnie.

"Can I keep these pictures overnight?" I asked Mr. O'Reilly, gesturing to Larry's graduation picture and a picture of Larry's son.

"Certainly," he said.

Promising to return them the next day, I borrowed the two pictures. When I got home, I put the photographs on my bed. A teenager, my son Lonnie came home from school and saw the pictures.

"Gee!" he said. "That guy looks just like me."

"You look like twins," I told my son. "That's Larry O'Reilly's son, and this is Larry." I pointed at the other picture.

"Mom," he exclaimed. "You look just like Larry!" I looked at Larry's graduation picture and placed my own high school graduation picture next to it, and I saw the similarity. It was unmistakable. In addition to our coloring, Larry and I held our heads the same way for the pictures. I certainly looked more like him than I did Margaret, yet people had long said that I looked like my birth mother.

The next day, I returned the photographs to Mr. O'Reilly, though I later regretted that I hadn't made copies of the photos before I returned them. Larry's father told me about his family—including the fact that some of Larry's sisters were music teachers—and I was pretty much in and out of his house for some time. Terribly disappointed that Larry was dead, I wished that I could have had an opportunity to meet him, and, later, I would have wanted to do a DNA test. Though I believed that Larry was my father, and that I had inherited my musical abilities from his family, I wasn't sure, and I did not want to tell his father of my suspicion until I had proof. But, as it happened, I never did tell him who I was, and I came to regret this.

I hired an attorney, Doug Head, a former Attorney General for the State of Minnesota, and his colleague Thomas Seifert. One of their most valuable contributions to my case was that they connected me with John Murphy, a former FBI agent who would also help and advise me.

In time, this remarkable trio would help me answer other questions and pursue different avenues of investigation, but in the beginning, I sought one thing: Mike's identity.

Before I could determine whether Mike or Larry was my father, I needed to know who Mike was. To that end, I set John Murphy loose on the investigation. Before long, he found it. Among all the records and reports and documents, there was a single instance where Mike's last name had not been blacked out. Though his family and their money, likely with the help of attorney, Henry Bank, had managed to expunge his record of any criminal history and censored the record with blackout nearly everywhere, they had not succeeded in retaining his anonymity forever. One document, which was never to be seen by human eyes again, contained the information. By agreement, I cannot reveal which record contained the information. The only important thing was that Murphy found it. "Mike" was Mitchell Osman of Minneapolis.

Osman had remained in Minneapolis. With a sparkling clean record, he married into another very wealthy family and moved to one of the wealthiest suburbs in Minneapolis, where he lived as a man of considerable means. He became a Minneapolis businessman with many commercial interests.

I wasn't surprised, but I felt blown away. The man who probably killed the Willow River baby—and would have killed me—was an upstanding citizen. A man of money and stature, a family man. A businessman. He had certainly strayed far as a teenager, into the seedy streets, bars, and motels of South Minneapolis. While Margaret was a woman with a secret in her past, Mike was a man who had hidden a secret life, an entire dark history and a side of himself that was not all fun and games. His young adulthood involved pregnant teenagers and dead babies in black canvas bags. Had Mitchell Osman really left that history behind, or was he still a man who strayed into the dreary neighborhoods on the wrong side of the tracks?

Even if he had outgrown the mistakes and indiscretions of his youth, it made me sick to think that such an immoral man might have been my father. If he was, I wondered what he felt as an adult. Did he care whether I was alive? Did he care that, at least, he had given me to a good family, who raised me with wholesomeness and love? Of course, I had no logical reason to think that he did care, and every reason to think that, with his money and means, he might still want me dead. But, still, I hoped that a part of him wondered about me. I even hoped that, maybe, a part of him actually felt guilty about what he had almost done to me. Maybe he even felt anguish about what he had possibly likely done to the Willow River baby.

I was desperate to know what kind of a man he was, and whether he cared at all. And I was prepared to accept that he might be as selfish and heartless as Margaret. If so, I knew what I would do. I would turn away from both of them and never look back.

Now that I had his name—Mitchell Osman—I prayed that Larry O'Reilly was my father so that I could forget about Mike. But I had to know. For my own safety and sanity, I had to be sure that Mike was not my father.

I gathered everything I knew about him and wrote all of it down, producing a dossier of about fifteen pages. Then, with the legal advice and support of my attorneys and my former FBI agent, I picked up the phone and called Mitchell Osman's place of business.

"I'm the daughter that you and Margaret had," I said boldly into the telephone. He did not speak. I heard nothing but dead silence on the other end of the phone. "Can we get together and talk?"

"Yes," he said. "Why don't we go to lunch?"

I agreed, and we made plans to meet.

I met him in the lobby of a posh restaurant, which he had suggested. The decor was very elegant. Though he had made a reservation for our luncheon, we waited for a table. In his early fifties, he was still very handsome and was extremely well dressed in a full three-piece silk suit with a beautiful tie and a crisp white shirt. As soon as I introduced myself, I handed him the dossier. I wanted him to know that I wasn't fooling around. While we stood there, he read every word before he looked up at me. "You've done your homework very well," he said.

The hostess was ready to seat us, so we followed her to a table that was almost in the dead center of the dining room. As we approached the table, Mike poured on the charm, helping me with my chair. As soon as we sat down, he asked if he could have the pleasure of ordering for me. I declined. After we ordered and the waiter left us alone, he looked at me.

"All right, then," he said. "What would you like to know?"

"Tell me about 1936," I requested.

He was soft-spoken and articulate. "I was a wild kid back in 1936," he said. "I had an affair with Margaret, but I wasn't the only boy that Margaret went out with. There were a lot of them." He seemed to be watching my reaction to see if he shocked me, which he did not. I did not speak or otherwise react, so he continued.

"I always thought someone else was your father, because I always used condoms and I thought they would protect me from getting her pregnant," he said. "But Margaret blamed me." Then he paused and looked at me before he asked, "Do you think I'm your father?"

"Margaret insisted that you were," I said. "Well, that's good enough for me."

As our meals arrived, the food was gorgeous and the service impeccable. Mike had perfect manners.

"Tell me about your family," he said politely. "Do you have a husband and children?" I told him a little bit about Richard and my sons, showing his pictures of them.

"I have three daughters," he said. "One is a police officer."

"Do I look like any of your daughters?"

"Maybe the middle one."

"What's Margaret's married name?" he asked me. I thought it a strange question.

"She married and has eight children," I said. "What's her last name?" he asked again.

"I can't tell you."

"Ah," he nodded. "Well, where does she live?"

I knew that he knew where she lived. I figured that he just wanted to see if I knew and that it was a ruse to make me think that they weren't in contact with each other. Then, the lies started to flow as if it was second nature.

"After Margaret became pregnant, I never saw her," he claimed. "I didn't even know that she was expecting until the police arrested me."

Of course, this was an obvious lie, as I knew that he had seen Margaret while she was in the hospital.

"What can you tell me about Agnes, the seamstress?" I asked. "She was a friend of yours in 1936."

"I've never heard of her," he said, though it was another lie. "How long have you known about yourself?"

"Since I was thirty-one years old," I said.

"And how long has Margaret known that you're alive?" he asked. "Since I was thirty-two years old," I said.

"She should have informed me that you are alive and well," he said, his brows twitching. A great actor, Mike also was an excellent liar, just like Margaret. "I always felt that the baby had met with a terrible end," he said. "And I figured that Margaret knew what happened to you. Have you gotten to know Margaret at all?"

"Yes," I said. "I have."

Suddenly, I didn't feel right about the meeting. I felt as though something was missing. Or wrong. I realized that I was sitting in a beautiful, first-class restaurant with a man who had wanted me dead, a man who had possibly killed another infant.

I felt an adrenaline rush. Mike had to have known that many people knew I was meeting him, so I knew that I was somewhat safe, but I wanted to get away from him.

"It's time for me to go," I blurted out, trembling.

Mike promptly got up, helped me with my chair, and walked with me out of the restaurant. He remained by my side as I walked to my car.

"You are lucky to be a lovely, intelligent, well-educated girl," he said. "I hope you will go home and feel good about yourself."

On top of all my fear, I started to cry. Mike leaned over and kissed me on my cheek. "Let's have lunch again sometime," he said.

I felt happy and safe to be driving home with no one in my rear view mirror.

# 20

## Attorneys

John Murphy, my FBI agent, tracked down Sheriff Hannes Rypkema some 40 years after the death of the anonymous Willow River baby. Rypkema told my investigator that he always felt the case had been hushed up and that Mike received preferential treatment from the police in 1936.

The police had had solid circumstantial evidence linking Mike to the dead baby. That evidence, which had never been dispelled, included a downtown Minneapolis drugstore clerk who had identified Mike and his friend as purchasers of the black bag—marked by varnish from the store shelves—in which the Willow River baby had been drowned. Further, the record had shown that Mike had many girlfriends in northern Minnesota, and that he had used an alias when registering at hotels in the area. Though Rypkema remained suspicious of Mike, he could not investigate all the leads to his satisfaction. Everything was hushed up and the Minnesota Department of Criminal Apprehension insisted that the sheriff turn over all of his files to them. In the end, Sheriff Rypkema remained very suspicious that Mike had gotten away with murder.

The official record supports this hunch. My attorneys and investigators agree that the official story does not appear to be on the up and up. Across the board, the city, county, and state jurisdictions—Minneapolis, Hennepin County, and the Minnesota Department of Criminal Apprehension—failed to pursue the investigation of Mike. Indeed, Mike was not charged in Minneapolis and the investigation was expunged from his record and, up in Pine County, when Sheriff Hannes Rypkema turned his investigation over to the state, those records disappeared and the investigation ended. Despite all the evidence, Mike got off scot-free. And there's no record anywhere of an investigation into the young woman who drove through the foggy night into the service station in Willow River Village with an infant in the back of her car, just hours before a baby was found drowned nearby.

By 1974, after spending a great deal of money and several years of my life investigating the case, I agreed with Sheriff Rypkema. But I went further. It was likely, I figured, that the mob had paid off the authorities in order to keep Mike in the clear. With the support of my attorney, Doug Head, I decided to make an appointment with Henry Bank, the attorney who had represented Margaret in 1936. Doug Head told me to be careful.

When I walked into the law offices of Henry H. Bank, I met a shady-looking man at the front desk. Despite the fact that he looked impeccable in a three-piece suit with a kerchief in his breast pocket, he looked rough, staring at me by way of a greeting. He didn't look like a typical legal secretary.

Mr. Bank emerged from his office and ushered me in. He wore a suit, also with a kerchief, but his necktie was tucked into a high, V-neck vest. Getting on in years, he had trimmed, thinning silver hair that grew from a receding hairline over oversized ears. I noticed at once that his pointy mouth seemed to say something about the authority he had enjoyed for decades. I felt scared to death. Though he looked like a mobster, he stared at me as if he'd seen a ghost.

Somehow, I sensed that he did, too. "Who sent you?" he asked.

As soon as he brought me into his office, his phone rang, so I sat in a chair facing his desk. I waited and listened as he talked into the phone, making an appointment with the caller. When he finally hung up, he looked at me and again turned red in the face.

"My name is Margaret Bolin," I lied. "And I wanted to talk to you." At least that part was true.

"I don't understand," he said. "Who are you?"

I knew that all attorneys kept a book listing all of their clients and dates. "I'd like you to check your little black book," I said, "and see who hired you in 1936."

Bank arose and walked through a door on the back wall of his office. It looked like he went into a walk-in closet, rather than another office. I figured he went somewhere to be private so that he could call his most notorious client, Mike Osman. He emerged about ten minutes later, claiming that he couldn't find anything about a case in 1936.

"Listen," I said, trying to sound confident and unafraid. "My attorney is Doug Head, and he knows I'm here, and why." I figured it was a good idea to let Bank know this, just in case he had anything unsavory in mind.

Bank looked at me with his piercing brown eyes, which were heavily burdened by bushy brows. He seemed to reconsider for a moment. "Who's your mother?" he asked, as if he'd remembered a second thought.

"Margaret Bolin," I said. "Surely you remember her?"

"Never heard of her," he said in a low, tight voice. Slowly, he stood up, parking all ten of his fingertips on the edge of his desk. His fingernails turned white as he pressed down onto them, and he glared at me. He seemed to be upset that I was there.

"You remember the case of the missing baby from General Hospital in 1936?" I asked, tentatively. "You represented Margaret, my mother. It was the biggest case of your career."

Bank's face turned red as he told me that he had never heard of Margaret Bolin or the case of the missing baby. "If you don't leave right now," he snarled, "I'm gonna throw you out!"

His posture was so harsh and unsettling that I suddenly felt very frightened and immediately took my leave. When I left, I noticed the same menacing black car following me.

Forty years after my birth in the century-old Minneapolis General Hospital, the building was scheduled to be demolished and replaced with the new and improved Hennepin County Medical Center. Before the wrecking ball destroyed the place of my illustrious disappearance, I wanted to see it, study it, and feel it, to wander its cool hallways and sneak up its granite stairs. I went inside to see what it was like.

I walked into the granite lobby and approached the grand information desk, where Violet Budd had been a receptionist those many years ago. About a dozen feet long, the stocky marble box of a desk was book-ended by a pair of marble columns, each topped with capitals of dark wood, ornately carved. Behind the desk, an alcove was finished with deep crown molding that divided the elegant, dark-wood ceiling from the stately walls, and above a dark wooden door an old wall clock with Roman numerals grandly accented the back wall.

To one side, I found the granite stairs. Up two flights, the stairs opened onto a main hallway that seemed to the width of the building, and I was near the middle. The walls were clean but dull and yellowing, and it was quiet, though the sound of my steps seemed lost and lonesome. I walked to my right, across an intersecting hallway and away from the elevators, and came to the nursery, which was in the middle of the floor. A smile came to my face as I imagined the loving Swedish nurses who had shown me so much care and kindness. Then, I walked down the quiet hallway and found the room, on the inside wall, where Margaret had spent so many consequential days of her teenage years, and I found the hallways where Mike and Margaret had talked, planning my death. The hair on the back of my neck stood up and I got cold chills.

Suddenly, I was desperate to leave, to get away from the place where my death had been plotted, where my life had been so close to ending before it had really begun. I felt as if I could see them—Margaret and Mike—talking about throwing my tiny body in Lake Calhoun, as if I wasn't a person, as if I wasn't human, as if I was nothing. I imagined the voices in the hallways of the hospital, busy with doctors and nurses in 1936, and felt sick.

My husband Richard wanted to move his home-building business to the Seattle area, and, since I was desperate for a change of scenery, I welcomed the move across the country. So, in the fall of

1977, we sold our home, packed up our lives, and moved to the Pacific Northwest with our sons, who were young adults by then.

The first thing we did in Seattle was find and join a new church. It was wonderful, and our church life helped us settle in with many new friends and a new life. Our church was very important to us, and Richard soon became an elder as I became the organist, playing for the church for the twenty years that we lived in Seattle. As always, I loved music, which was a big part of my life wherever I lived. I played for many weddings and funerals, and continued to sing barbershop harmony with Sweet Adelines. We made many new friends, were very happy, and I felt as if the move saved my life, moving me away-both physically and emotionally-from so many bad memories.

Being in Seattle was the best thing I could have done, because the change of scenery helped me to forget about Margaret and Mike so that I could heal and get on with my life. I didn't completely forget, though. Sometimes, when the church was empty, I would sit in a pew, talk to God, and just cry. Prayer always helped me, as did the pastors, who knew my story. So, for the most part, I had a new life and I got better as I grew away from Margaret and her family.

The first pastor in whom I confided was Pastor John Luthens, a wonderful man who would later become a hospital chaplain. He comforted me, assuring me that God had already forgiven me for lying to Margaret's family. He told me that God loved me very much. I still pray every night for God's forgiveness, for the lies that I was forced to tell.

My attorneys, Douglas Head and Thomas Seifert, got in touch with me. They informed me that DNA testing had changed and technology was now to the point that the Minneapolis Memorial Blood

Bank was doing this testing. The scientific validity of the testing had been established and, at that time, the test was reliable in establishing parentage. Further, Minnesota Laws of Civil Procedure allowed me to get a court order to compel Mike to take such a test. The law also stated that an "illegitimate child shall inherit" from a person who had been determined to be the father of a child in a paternity proceeding before a court of competent jurisdiction.

I did not want any inheritance, but Mike Osman did not know that. I was concerned that he might think that an inheritance was what I had in mind, though all I wanted was to know, for sure, who I was. Doug Head suggested that I undergo the test—and have Mike Osman do the same—to prove once and for all whether he was my father or not.

Doug Head sent Mike a letter informing him that I wanted him to undergo a DNA blood test that would definitively establish or rule out his paternity. Attorneys advised Mike that, if he refused, an order compelling a blood test could probably be obtained under rule 35 of Minnesota Rules of Civil Procedure. Mike's attorneys further informed him that I was seriously considering just such a lawsuit, despite the deleterious effects that such an action might have on all concerned-including myself. While I hoped to avoid it, and prayed that Mike would agree to a private blood test without me having to force him into it, I was prepared to force the issue.

Mike had his attorney write a letter, requesting that my attorneys spell out the case law that showed that a judge can issue an order requiring a person who has denied paternity to submit to a DNA blood test. My attorneys submitted the law, under Rule 35:01 of the Minnesota Rules of Civil Procedure.

His attorneys said that, under certain conditions, they might consent and Mike might agree to have the test, but they would first need to obtain a binding agreement from me with instructions that:

1. *A submission to the requested test would end any further inquiries affecting Mitchell Osman, including any type of notoriety involving Mike, his relatives, or his associates.*
2. *There would be no further inquiries or notoriety involving the mother.*
3. *No legal proceedings would be commenced to establish paternity for any other reason involving this matter.*
4. *I would agree to relinquish any claim that I may contend to have under any laws of inheritance, dissent, or distribution.*

I agreed to all of these conditions.

Finally on September 12, 1977, Mike's attorney informed my attorneys that, with necessary and adequate legal documents completed, Mike would submit to the blood tests.

My attorneys drew up a lengthy agreement that essentially stated that Mike would agree to the tests with a guarantee from me that I would not sue Mike to establish paternity, and that I would waive and release Mike and his heirs, personal representatives, and successors from all rights of inheritance with regard to him or his estate. But the first paper named him as "Al Osman." I immediately told my attorney to record it as Mike's name—Mitchell Osman.

On October 11, 1977, Mike signed the agreement and his attorneys sent a copy to my attorney at the law firm of Head & Truhn.

When Mike appeared at the Minneapolis Memorial Blood Bank, he produced a photo identification and his blood was collected.

On January 16, 1978, the result of the DNA test was sent to attorney Thomas Seifert of Head & Truhn. The interpretation from the test protocol established that Mike Osman was *not* my father and that he, in no way, could have contributed to my gene group. The test had provided solid evidence—proof of non-paternity in this case. Mike was definitely not my father.

That was all I needed. Finally, I could close this chapter of my life. The man who had wanted me dead, the man who would have thrown me in a lake, the man who probably threw an innocent infant into the Willow River, was not my father. He was not my blood.

It had been a long and arduous ordeal, a miserable journey and a desperate question, and all I felt was relief. My fears of Mike were allayed. Finally, I could be content with what I believed—that Larry O'Reilly was my father.

The whole encounter was strange, though, that, while Mike was not my father, he obviously feared me. I'll never know for sure, but I believe his fear had something to do with the Willow River baby.

# 21

# Family

In 1986, I was about to turn fifty. As that momentous birthday neared, I heard that the Minneapolis newspaper was going to do a fiftieth-anniversary story about the missing baby and the fact that I had been "found." A reporter for the Minneapolis paper discovered that my mother was still alive. In an effort to get as much story as he could, he told my relatives the story of my birth. Newspaper reporters do not care how much they hurt people.

The paper had supposedly found me from a Minneapolis General Hospital report. I wanted nothing to do with it and tried to stop the story, and I told the reporter that I was not the missing baby. However, behind my back and without my consent, the reporter got Margaret to do a DNA test, and Margaret had told the reporter that my DNA was already on file with the Minneapolis Memorial Blood Bank. It seems criminal that the blood bank would betray my privacy so blatantly—and to the press—and I considered filing suit against them for providing a confidential report. However, being in Seattle and removed from the situation, I didn't want to deal with it. I kept my distance. That also meant that, while the paper had no idea what the whole truth was, I wasn't about to tell them. I didn't even follow the fiftieth anniversary story when it ran in the paper. That year, I had one last bit of trouble with Margaret's family. They found out that my mother was alive—that she had been alive all along—and they weren't happy about it.

When I first met Margaret in 1968, I protected my mother, Inga Hermanson, by telling all of the Bolins that my mother had died, that she had told me her secret on her death bed. For nearly twenty years, I continued to protect her by maintaining that story. Although I'd grown close to some of Margaret's siblings—my aunts and uncles— when they found out in 1986 that I had lied about my mother's death, they were angry with me. They did not seem to understand why I protected my mother. Despite the affection I had with Rosie, Shirley, Betty and the others, we had a serious falling out when they learned that my mother had been alive all those years. I suppose that they thought that Inga Hermanson had actually kidnapped me—stolen me from Margaret—as if she would have been a doting mother were it not for the woman who took me. By some stretch of wishful thinking, I guess they developed an alternate reality, in which I might have turned Inga Hermanson in to the police, and she would have gone up on charges all those years later. Or, perhaps, Margaret and her siblings would have publicly tarred and feathered her, holding her up to ridicule for some horrendous crime.

They conveniently seem to forget—or dismiss—the inconvenient fact that Margaret, herself, was the criminal, not the mother who raised me. They did not know the whole story—that I would have died in Lake Calhoun before I was two weeks old had my fate been left in Margaret's hands. They thought the best of their oldest sister, believing that she was a good mother, believing that my presence had vindicated her. They did not know that I wasn't kidnapped, as they'd always thought, but that Margaret had given me away like an old hand-me-down that was otherwise destined for the trash.

I have wondered what they would have done if they had been in my place. I kept my mother's identity under wraps, sheltering her from the Bolins, keeping her safe from their scrutiny and their blame, because I knew that they could not see the truth. I knew that they had to blame my mother because it would have been to awful to blame Margaret for what she had, in fact, done.

In the end, with Margaret's siblings angry at me for protecting my mother. I felt as if they were saying that they agreed with what Margaret did. It was akin to thinking that they thought I would have been better off dead. Had I survived, I thought, they should have been grateful to my mother for taking me.

Ultimately, it became clear to me that, as much as they accepted me, it really only went so far. I felt as if they didn't care if I existed or not—just like the Willow River baby. Although Margaret had said that the dead infant was her child, they had not claimed her for burial, but allowed her to be buried in a pauper's grave.

The irony is that it is only because of my mother and me that the Bolins learned that Margaret's baby wasn't dead, that the Willow River baby was not Margaret's child. The truth is that, without my mother's actions, Margaret's baby *would* have been dead, and without my actions, her family never would have known the truth.

Today, it's been more than forty years since I found out, more than forty years since I told Margaret and her family that I am alive. For many of those years, the Bolin family paraded me around like some bonfire of truth, like a walking and talking polygraph test. They celebrated my life, but not because they missed me or loved me or anguished over what had become of me. They celebrated my life only because my existence—my survival—was valuable to them. I was Margaret Bolin's vindication. And until her dying day, she remained a selfish and narcissistic girl—a woman who cared nothing about me, but only about what I meant to her.

In 1968, when the sordid reality struck me out of the blue, I felt that I had a responsibility to clear Margaret's name. I felt like the truth was the one thing that I owed to my birth mother. I stepped forward in order to allow her to say, "See? I told you I didn't do it! It was the nurse in blue, just like I said!"

But, if I had it to do over again, I would not have cleared her name because she turned the truth around on me.

Margaret is not the hero! Margaret is not the one who saved my life. Inga Hermanson is the woman who saved me from Margaret and Mike. She is the hero. She is the mother in my story.

All I got in return was that her family vilified Inga, and treated me like an outsider. Once they learned that my mother was alive and that I had protected her since 1968, they turned their backs on me and in deference to Margaret. In defending her, they had condemned me, yet again.

As I kept my distance from the Bolin family, I received the following letter, which Margaret's daughter Laura sent to me:

*Dear Lorene,*

*Forgive me for the not fancy paper but its 3:30am and so as not to disturb my family I grabbed what I could find in the semi-darkness here. I have laid awake for an hour and a half thinking about you and came to the conclusion that maybe a letter (if they'll forward it) will help me sleep and, perhaps, let you know that I do care that you have been hurt so deeply by someone I love dearly. I only wish I could sit and talk to you. Your letter told me so much and yet I could kick myself for not reaching out to you before the miles were so many between us. If only I could sit down with you now.*

*Perhaps, as you know, I have probably been the closest to my mother and my dad of all the kids. I'm not sure of what things you know but there is a point in my life that made that possible. While no one knows any other persons exactly, I feel I know Mother better than any other person alive on earth here. While I rarely agree with their viewpoints, morals, or whatever, I have come through treacherous efforts to accept them for what they are and not to judge them—for, as we know, that is only God's power to judge. I know it is so hard perhaps even impossible for you because the way you see things and all that happened in those years (good, bad, and sad) have made me love them for what they are. "Memories are the most wonderful gifts God has given us," I think. Not only are we able to enjoy life at the moment, but time and time again through the power of our fabulous minds. My most important philosophy in life is God lets nothing happen without a reason— nothing.*

*A couple weeks ago [my son] Casey had emergency surgery for a suspected tumor in his left cheek. Lorene, this was one of the most heartbreaking moments in my life. [My children] Corky and Carrie have never had anything serious wrong with them. As unreasonable as it all seemed, I know God had his reasons for this baby to suffer like he did. But I know it was a gift of God that it was not a tumor and a gift of God the surgeon made this softball—size cheek normal again.*

*What I guess I'm trying to get at is, right or wrong, accept it and at some time God will let you know the why of it all. And accept my mother as she is and for what she is—right or wrong. As far as you wanting things made right by the law, I couldn't agree with you more. But she has only one person to answer to: herself.*

*God has known all these years the truth. He has not condemned her for what her fellow man misunderstood. He was able to sit back and watch this beautiful baby grow up to be a beautiful talented woman. It's hard to understand but remember all that's happened, your childhood, all of it had made you the person you are today. You had a musical talent recognized young enough where you were able to develop it to bring you and others so much joy. Be thankful for what you are—a beautiful person in and out.*

*If your life wasn't the way it was, you perhaps would have never met wonderful Dick. Stop and think of all the happiness he has brought you—especially two terrific sons. Can't you admit as life goes on the love bond grows stronger between people because of time. You love him more in spite of himself, right? He's human. He has faults, but you've accepted him as is. But I think it's hard for you to accept Mother because you didn't have the formative years with her. I know a mother and a husband are two entirely different things but I just can't think of any other comparison. I'm not even sure I'm making any sense at all. My mind is so full of things I'd like to say, but it's hard to write them down and know if I'm coming across with what I mean.*

*Though I know it matters little at all, my brothers and sisters were very happy to meet you, Dick, Lonnie and Ronnie. I never heard any of the kids (brothers and sisters) say a word against any of you. We liked you all very much.*

*What wasn't there to like? You know your little family are terrific people and fun to be with.*

*Yes, we were surprised. I'd be a liar if I were to say not. You look more like Mother than any of us. She couldn't deny you if she tried. No one, I'm sure, can honestly know how you feel. I'm sure you have been hurt deeper than most of us will ever be hurt. I'm sure you missed what most of a lot of people take for granted. I'm sure you have needs and desires that you cannot fulfill but only she (Mother) could, but we don't know if she ever will.*

*My heart reaches out to you, Lorene. Truly, like I said, I wish I could walk with you. I know I could help you some at least. I'm sorry I didn't reach out to you when it was possible. There is a saying that keeps crossing my mind as I think of you and Mother's situation. I don't know it exactly but it's something like, "I am I and you are you and if our roads should reach and meet together, then that is beautiful."*

*You and Mother are each your own persons. Don't ask her down your path and yet don't follow hers. I feel so sure your paths will come together at some time. I know Mother is not a verbal person who shows or tells how she feels easily. That is just the way she is. She enjoyed being with you. She told me this. While I don't like to tell what others have confided in me, don't put yourself down. She does care for you. Maybe it's not what you expected so she hasn't let you down. But you have let yourself down. I'm sure she has said very hurtful things to you but she has also done the very same to me and I say this honestly. No one can hurt you deeper than those you care about.*

*One last thing…Mother and Dad, I feel, are alcoholics. For whatever reason, this has become their way of life. Really, to me, it is so sad that anyone should have to depend on any chemical for their ups and downs or in-betweens. They have hurt me so deeply so often when they have been drinking. I do know how you feel there: But, once again, we mustn't judge them, right? As hard as it is, we mustn't.*

*Over my sink is my prayer of St. Francis of Assisi. I'm mailing it with this letter. I would be very pleased and honored if you'd keep it. I turned to this saint so often when so down. I'm sure you know the prayer too, but just take my well-worn little card when this has all got you down and, remember, when I was as low as you can get, it's lifted me up somehow. Another saint I've come to rely on is St. Jude. When all else fails, St. Jude will work a miracle for us.*

*Since your letter, I've thought of you so much but as I said I've been all wrapped up in Casey's surgery and his care once home. But I still apologize for not trying to get to you sooner. Please don't punish me by cutting yourself off from us completely. Wouldn't you be punishing yourself, too?*

*If you were to send me your address, I promise I wouldn't give it to anyone without your permission first. I swear that to you. I would really like to know where you are and how you are. I was happy to hear the weather is helping you there. Who knows? Perhaps that asthma was part of God's plan for you to not stay here. But that doesn't mean we can't be friends, does it? Many of my friends from Minneapolis I feel closer to now than when I was there.*

*Please, at least use my letter as food for thought. Though I am younger than you, there have been many struggles in my life and I have come to know myself and what helps me well. Perhaps you're thinking, Boy, thank God this is the last I have to hear from this kook. But, you see, I don't know what you think, unfortunately. I do want you to know I do care how you feel about this and how I liked you for what you were when I met you.*

*Whether either of us faces it, we are half-sisters. Please think a little over what I said. I hope you will send me your address on the conditions I mentioned. If I hear nothing in the next couple of weeks, I will understand. Whatever you do, I will not hang anything where I removed my St. Francis prayer, but will think of you when I look there.*

*Wishing you the best,*

*Laura*

*P.S. I'm not sure if you knew Barbie had a baby girl a healthy 8 ½ pounder. It was before Christmas.*

I felt as if Margaret, her siblings, and her children had no sense of reality, of the truth that had been my life since 1968. Reading Laura's letter, I felt as if the truth did not matter. The newspaper accounts, the county files, police reports, and every other scrap of evidence that spoke the testimony of history—that I was to have been drowned in Lake Calhoun—seemed to mean nothing to the Bolins. It was as if I was welcome in their family, as long as I did not speak the truth—or ask for it.

This was my chance to reply to Laura:

*Laura,*

*I don't remember if I answered your letter or not. The problem I had with your mother was that she wouldn't even tell me my father's name. I begged her for years for this. I had to find out on my own with DNA tests. She would call me on the phone drunk, but even then she wouldn't tell me. I don't think that, under the circumstances, that was too much to ask. If she didn't know, that's all she would have had to say. I understand that Jennifer eventually asked her for her father's name and your mother told her.*

*I know that none of you understand why I protected my mother who raised me. Well, she was a fantastic mother and, if you read this book, you*

204

*will know that she saved my life. I was very fortunate to have the parents that I did. I was raised in church and gave my musical abilities to God. I was the church organist for over thirty years in Seattle along with singing and teaching little girls to become church singers. Your family hurt me when your mother died. An uncle-in-law let me know or I would have never known. Like you said, we're half-sisters. What happened? I also was not listed as being her daughter. Perhaps you all thought I wanted part of her estate, which I did not.*

*Lorene*


When Margaret was pregnant with me, her mother Barbara was also pregnant. Six months after I was born and gone, Barbara had her baby, a daughter, and they gave her the name they had given me: Shirley.

As a young child, Shirley Bolin was hit by a vehicle and she was permanently injured, walking stooped over until she finally got a prosthesis that helped her walk perfectly. Shirley and her husband Henry remained our friends, in spite of all the rest of the family. Were it not for Henry, I would never have known that Margaret was very sick with emphysema, and that she died in June of 1995. Henry even sent me a sympathy card. A wonderful and decent man, Henry became a very good friend of Richard's. With Henry's death, all family connections are severed, forever, I hope.

The Bible says that only the truth can set us free. I tried to make that work for me, but dealing with liars made it pretty hard. So many times, I went and sat in an empty church and cried. My pastor, Pastor Schultz, tried to help me, suggesting that I ask God to forgive my natural family, which I have done. He also told me to learn to love myself, and he reminded me that God loves me. We had lunch now and then, and I know that the pastor was keeping an eye on me. He told me to go and pray in church, just as I had been doing, whenever I felt the need and for as long as I needed to.

Church, my family, and the distance from Minneapolis were helping me recover. After years of praying and going to church, with the privilege of giving my music to God, the past didn't seem to matter much. I had a wonderful husband and two great sons, as well as a thriving career and music always in my life. I was very happy with what I was doing, but sometimes the past would sneak back, causing tears to run down my cheeks. Some wounds just never heal. I continued to wish, desperately, that my mother had never told me about 1936.

# 22

# The Right Thing

Though I learned forty years ago that my mother and father were not my biological parents, I continue to this day to debate the value of the revelation of the truth. Am I better off for knowing? Is Margaret better off, now that her family knows? With the exception of the first ten days of my life, Margaret and I have lived in different worlds, so the considerations about the virtue of the truth are completely different for each of us.

When Margaret was fifteen, she had the mind of a child and the morals of a rabbit. Though she was sexy and streetwise as a young teenager, she was still a child, a girl, with a fifth-grade education. Barely literate, she had little practical knowledge about anything like work, learning a trade, working for money, or anything like that. The only thing she knew was seduction, and she knew it well.

Why Margaret was so sexually sophisticated at such a young age is unknown, but the fact is that she was, very much so. And while she certainly chose to use that sophistication to manipulate men and to get what she wanted, in many ways the men who were in her life and who crossed her path turned that manipulation back on her, in spades. With no idea of her personal worth, Margaret sold herself cheap. While she wanted a husband and a home, love and luxury, she instead got a fraction of that, little trinkets, tokens of affection, while the men took all they could get their hand on. They trifled with the naïve and beautiful young girl, used her for sex, and paid her in dime store toys. Though the legal authorities condemned Margaret and her men, she was never seen as a victim, was never protected. The men and the system victimized her, and turned her into the woman who she became.

Did Margaret's life suddenly go down the drain when everyone thought she'd played a role in the disappearance and death of her baby? No. Given her delusions of grandeur and sense of entitlement, she was destined to suffer from unrealized fantasies. Given her dysfunctional childhood and her distaste for working, she was doomed for unhappiness and poverty. Given her taste for beer and the genetic hand that she'd been dealt, she could hardly have avoided becoming an alcoholic. And given her logic about using sex to get a fraction of what she wanted from men, she was bound to have additional unwanted pregnancies. Considering all that she did to mess up her own life, it is no surprise that Margaret ended up an unhappy, poor, alcoholic mother. She had every opportunity to change her ways after the first time that she was sent to the Sauk Center Training School for Delinquent Girls. She did not learn from that experience, but carried on, walking briskly through her life in the fast lane. Realistically, in the big picture of such a life, the incident of the missing baby and Margaret's three-year confinement must have seemed like just another episode of her teen angst.

This is not to say that she did not suffer for those thirty years, while people thought that she'd killed her baby. No doubt, she did suffer. But that pain would have been the result of Margaret's lies, not my mother's secret. So this begs the question: Would Margaret have suffered less if my mother had come forward earlier? Probably not. She might not have ended up in the Sauk Center School, but, then again, she'd been there before and likely would have ended up there again, anyway, for something else. And Margaret still would have been alcoholic, poor, promiscuous, and fertile.

Her life, had the truth been known, probably would have been no better, though it certainly could have been worse. Margaret constantly flirted with disaster. For example, her sisters told me stories about coat-hanger abortions at Margaret's house. Margaret may well have been the "patient" in some such procedures, since she never wanted as many children as she had and certainly would not have welcomed more. Given the drunkenness in her marriage—and lack of reliable birth control—Margaret would have had few alternatives to more babies, regardless of the death rate suffered by desperate women in "back-room" abortions.

As it was, after my disappearance, Margaret produced a large brood-a family that she never really wanted. The oldest child after me was Patty, who was always rather cool and unfriendly toward me. Her husband eventually ran off with a younger woman, taking most of their money, and she ended up divorced. Jennifer was next. Looking quite a lot like me, Jennifer was the one who was the product of an affair while Margaret's husband Frank was away in the military. Then came Bob, one of Margaret's favorites. He was very athletic and worked for a pharmaceutical company in Minneapolis. Laura was the next child, who became pregnant as a teenager. Interestingly, Margaret threw her out of the house. Laura lived with one of Margaret's sisters for a while, and later married the father of her baby, so Margaret finally took her back in. Barbie was the next of Margaret's children. For a while, I had a good relationship with her, and even gave her a baby shower when she was pregnant. But, like most of her siblings, she turned her back on me when they found out that my mother was alive. The next child was Mike, who was a teenager when we met him. He was very handsome and, later, when he got married, we were invited to his wedding. Nicholas, like Mike, was very good looking and a teenager when we met him. Sarah, a child when we met her, was Margaret's constant companion, like a security blanket. She was always there, so I couldn't talk about my story or my father with Margaret.

These are my siblings, my half-brothers and half-sisters. One of them, Jennifer, is no more Frank's daughter than I am, and yet she is in the family while I am an outsider. Like a piece of trash, a throw-away baby, I am of no use to them. When I provided Margaret's vindication, I was part of the family. But, when they found out about the woman who raised me—the wonderful woman who saved me from Margaret, the upstanding woman who made me the person I am today—they turned their backs to me, as if I owed them something.

A significant irony is that Margaret was a terrible parent, while I was fortunate to be raised by a kind and disciplined mother. More like a pal than a parent to her children, Margaret was extremely lenient and always tried to be one of the kids, having fun with them. In the end, she never changed, but was always childlike herself. I thank God for looking out for me when Inga Hermanson walked down that corridor and took me into her arms. I am eternally grateful that she saw me as a child of God.

Margaret, on the other hand, lived in her own little world. While her husband worked nights at the Hennepin County Jail, Margaret would walk down to a local tavern for a few drinks. But she never associated with their neighbors, saying that she didn't believe in that. If she caught Frank talking with a neighbor—just engaging in friendly chit-chat—Margaret would cuss and yell at Frank, reminding him that "I don't believe in that!"

Margaret had a convenient recollection of the past, which did not include the fact that she plotted with Mike to drown her unwanted newborn in Lake Calhoun. Given this slip of memory, Margaret did not tell her children the truth about what happened. They never knew that she had consented to my murder, that Inga Hermanson had heard them talking about their plan, and that they gave me to her. Perhaps Margaret's other children believed that Inga had actually kidnapped me, tore me from Margaret's loving arms while the young mother lay heartbroken in her hospital bed. Ignorant of the truth, they listened to their mother's version of events, rather than mine.

They had no way of knowing that Margaret and Mike had planned murder—infanticide—and were spared by Inga, whom they swore to secrecy. More than four decades after I walked into their lives, they still refuse to believe the truth, my truth.

And, all these years later, I continue to wage my own war, an endless internal debate inside my mind: Should I have stayed away from the Bolins? Should I have kept my mother's secret to myself? Or was it worth it to meet my biological mother, to tell her family that I was alive? Was it the right thing to do, coming forward and vindicating her?

In the end, I feel deep regret and firm resolve that I should not have allowed myself to be paraded around so that Margaret could say, "See? I didn't kill my baby!"

In allowing Margaret to use me for her vindication, I let her treat me as if I was not valuable and precious for who I was, but for *what* I was. She objectified me by making me her vindication—nothing more.

It's interesting that the only time in my entire life when I have felt less valuable as a human being is with regard to Margaret. After all, she is the woman who had the capacity to throw away her own baby, or to let her boyfriend do so. For most of us, it is incomprehensible that a mother—however young she was—could agree to such a horror, much less to help plan it. But Margaret, with her inflated sense of self-importance, must regard the rest of us as lesser beings. That can be the only explanation for a woman, who could dispose of a newborn because it was inconvenient, and who could treat her grown daughter as if her only value was as a testament to her mother's humanity.

As a Christian, I believe in doing the right thing, and I thought that clearing Margaret's name was the right thing to do. But, if I could live this part of my life over again, I would never introduce myself to Margaret or her family. I would have stayed away and investigated from afar, leaving her to live the life she created for herself. I believe that God would forgive me for that.

Still, learning the truth of my life has caused me a great deal of suffering. In 1968, before my mother told me about my birth mother, I was a happy, healthy person, a strong, self-assured and proud woman in charge of myself and as I went about conquering the world.

When my mother told me the story about my first weeks of life, I lost the essence of myself. Although my parents had taught me a priceless sense of self-worth, it was instantly gone when I learned that I had been unwanted, that I was to have been disposed of like garbage. Compounding that reality of being regarded as worthless, I struggled with my identity; I was not really a good, church-going woman, the only child of my hardworking Norwegian parents, but the bastard daughter of a promiscuous teenage alcoholic who had no morals or character. I was devastated. I did not know who or what I was, as my self-assurance and self-worth were gone. I felt destroyed.

The revelations that my mother shared with me changed me forever. I knew that I would never be the same again, and I felt bad about that. I wanted to have my life back, to go back to being me, but I knew that I could not. I was damaged, and I always would be. It took some time, but I was finally able to revive some of my self-assurance, which helped me to push forward and conduct an investigation of the past. But, for the rest of my life, I will not be the same woman I was. And I will probably always wish that my mother had not told me.

Am I so different from other adopted children? Not really. While my biological mother was capable of condoning the death of her baby, that's about the only aspect of my "adoption" that makes it particularly unique. The fact is that many birth mothers are like Margaret— young, unwed, promiscuous, delinquent, addicted to alcohol or drugs, and otherwise dysfunctional. And many adoptive families are as good as mine—family-centered, religious, healthy, hard-working, and otherwise wholesome.

I suffered a great deal when I learned that my "real" parents did not live up to the ideals and standards with which I was raised; the gap between my upbringing and my heritage-has been very hard for me to accept.

Among those who have been adopted, I do not believe that I am alone in feeling that this knowledge causes a great burden, a sorrow and shame that offers little on the other side to tip the scale. I feel strongly that adoption records should be sealed so that adopted children never learn that they were adopted. I realize that this view seems old-fashioned, but I have yet to hear a good reason that justifies telling a child the truth, which may do little more than inflict pain, self-doubt, and worse. Expectations—which are usually based on fantasies—become disappointments. Once we learn that we have biological parents, we automatically try to include them in the emotional equation of our lives.

I look at this stranger—my birth mother—juxtaposed by my parents who raised me, and I have to reconcile all those feelings. I suddenly had two different lives, two identities. One mother I didn't remember or know, the other I have always called Mother. One gave me life, and the other valued that life enough to nurture it and teach me how to live it. One gave me a nationality, while the other gave me the love of a family. One gave me my genetics and seeds of talent, while another gave those seeds the sustenance and support they needed to bloom. One gave me up, while the other held me close, protected me, dried my tears.

We—adopted children—know who loves us. The parents who raised us are the only parents that matter. Better we should live the lives they gave us and not stop to wonder about or try to find biological parents who gave us away.

That is a journey I wish I had never taken. When adoptive parents tell their children that they are adopted, it makes those children curious about the unknown, about realities that are possibly best left alone.

Such knowledge may cause these sons and daughters to search—endlessly, sometimes—for their "real" parents, though what they find will be strangers, who are living their own lives with their own families, an exclusive club to which the adopted child was not welcome.

The past is past and things change, but the reality is always there for the child who was given away. *They got rid of me.* And there is always the chance that the child will be rejected again.

Although it is fashionable to reunite adoptive families, the problem is that they cannot start over. The child cannot forget the adoption, and the parents can't go back and raise the child, so these reunions are extremely complex. Simply finding and meeting birth parents doesn't make the child's original rejection go away. The wounds still exist and probably always will, and the complexity of the hurt will require ever more complex healing. That is not easy.

The truth does not always set you free. In my case, my campaign of investigation took years and cost many thousands of dollars. In the end, I am very sorry that I ever allowed myself involvement with Margaret and her family and, if I had it to do over again, I would have investigated from a distance, never letting Margaret know about me. Better yet, I do wish I had never known. The truth should have remained hidden forever. I was perfectly happy not knowing the real story of my birth, and I wish I had never known it.

# 23

# WILLOW RIVER

August 18, 2011 was a nice sunny day. Richard and I drove the ninety miles from the Twin Cities up to the town of Willow River. As we drove, I couldn't help but visualize the 1936 convoy of cars—filled with reporters, police, attorneys and my birth mother, Margaret—making that same drive during the state's greatest heat wave. I thought of Margaret on that fateful drive, as she would be looking at a dead baby, sobbing that the girl was her own child. Looking out the window as the Land of Lakes whizzed past, I felt somber and, yet, full of purpose and determination.

Willow River is a town of just a few streets laid out in a grid between Interstate 35 to the east and county highway 61 to the west. The two highways bend toward each other like an hourglass figure, which is cinched at the waist by a three-thousand foot belt formed by county highway 43. Just west of the town, the Willow River winds its way through the gentle countryside.

Arriving in Willow River, we drove past City Hall, which looked more like a post office and fire station in a low-slung building with a stone fence. Driving past a few houses, we crossed Church Street, aptly named for the small white church on the corner, and turned right on Main Street, just past the Post Office—another low-lying, rock-faced building.

Main Street was as quiet and sleepy as the highway was. We passed the school and then Main Street ended at Lake Street and we turned right. Just up the road, we saw another white church, this one at the corner of Lake and Church. St. Mary the Virgin Catholic Church was a prim and small church that sat on a manicured expanse of lawn, with headstones scattered in the cemetery beyond the church. Immediately, we met Marge Leonard and Vickie Whitehouse.

They had heard the story of the Willow River baby and we discussed it briefly. Both of them expressed what should have happened to the killer, and Richard and I agreed. They called Dave Kliniski, the head of the cemetery association, and he immediately left his business to come and help us to find the grave. While we waited for him, bells chimed from the church's steeple.

In my hand, I held a printout of a gravesite map that I had found online. The document had said that the "Unknown baby girl" had died on August 13, 1936 and was buried at Sunnyside Cemetery at St. Mary's Church, in section #1, Lot 326. Since it had been a pauper's burial in a potter's field, none of the graves was marked, so Dave brought a magnetic rod that could detect the iron grave markers, which were buried about four inches under the sod.

Soon, a city employee named Mike Cisar came and helped us.

We found the right area, and Dave waved his magnetic rod over the grass. In a second, it detected metal, so we dug into the grass for a few minutes and found the marker number. We were close, but it was the wrong number. Continuing, Dave located another iron marker but this, too, wasn't the right grave. When Dave detected metal again, we dug and found it: Number 326.

I was so touched to have the help and support of Marge and Vickie, and was even more thrilled and amazed that Dave and Mike—on the spur of the moment and in the middle of their busy lives—came out to help us. They had no knowledge of my story or the story of the Willow River baby, and yet they helped us, persisting until we found the right grave. It meant a lot to me that they would do that, and I consider all four of them to be my friends. We will never forget what they did to help us that day.

While chimes rang out from the little white church, everyone left so that Richard and I could be alone. I sat near the grave under a huge white pine tree and started to cry, thinking about how the baby had been killed, gasping for air. Who could do such a thing?

I thought about Margaret, who identified the dead baby as her own, while all of the General Hospital nurses were certain that the two babies were not the same. Claiming the baby as hers, Margaret committed an unforgivable mistake and lie that allowed authorities to forget the case. After Margaret's statement, the officials would not even try to find out who drowned the baby. Still, if Margaret claimed that the baby was hers, her family should have claimed the body and given it a proper burial. I felt sad and disappointed that they hadn't done the right thing, that they had turned their backs on her. And, in the end, I feel a special kinship with the Willow River baby. While we might have been sisters, we are not, but I feel as if we are spiritually linked by our stories. Nobody wanted her, either.

Richard and I had bought a small headstone, which he retrieved from the car. He fixed a double iron stake behind the headstone so it could be securely driven into the ground, and then he pounded the marker down into the earth. We put a spray of colorful flowers next to the marker. As the sun was getting low to the west, I took a deep, slow breath—in and out—and then I sighed. It was such a beautiful setting, the little white church, singing to us with its chimes, and the towering white pine tree overlooking the precious baby's grave. Richard wrapped his arms around me and we looked at the headstone:

## IF LOVE COULD HAVE SAVED YOU,
## YOU WOULD HAVE LIVED FOREVER

We could feel her presence, watching us from Heaven. I felt a connection with her, a bond across the years and through the dirt, as if she was there, with me that afternoon. I felt her asking us why she had died before she even had a chance to live, why she didn't have a mother's love. I felt as if she watched over us, there beside her grave, as if she was grateful that we cared enough to find her. I hope that she was pleased with what we did.

It was a sad day and hard to leave her grave, with her tiny body buried a few feet below the soft grass, but we wanted to go see the river. We drove the short distance from the cemetery to the river. From the road, we could see the deep, dark water of the river, just next to the road, and we found the island, about two-hundred feet through the scrubby trees, shrubs, and grasses. We realized that the black canvas bag could easily have been tossed into the cold water from a car on the road, and I felt a chill at the heart of the person who could weigh down a bag with magazines, stuff a baby into it, and throw her into the river to choke and die. She was alive when the bag sailed into the river, shocked and uncomprehending as the cold water smothered the life out of her.

With heavy hearts, we left Willow River and drove back to Minneapolis. We plan to return to Willow River every year and put fresh flowers on that precious baby's grave.


I will not forget her. For some reason, I feel connected to the Willow River baby. Maybe we are half-sisters. I'll never know, but I love that baby, anyway. The day will come when we're both in Heaven and I hope that we will be best friends.

Now, in the dead of winter, as the soft snow falls on Minnesota and Wisconsin, I know that snowflakes rest on the grave of the Willow River baby, covering it gently and silently. I know that the snow hushes all, and that the merciful Father alone can make it fall. The Willow River baby still sleeps, with a silence sweet and deep.

It would be three weeks later when this baby came to me in my dreams, I asked her what she wanted, she was wearing a wretched ragged blue dress and was crying. I asked her where she was, she didn't know, I told her to go to light. She didn't know, I told her to go to the light to Jesus and that she would be home. She said okay, and in a ray of light she was gone. When I woke up the next morning, I was quite shaken about what had happened. I knew that it was only a dream, but it seemed so real. If she went home to Jesus that made me feel good about the experience.

Two weeks later the baby came again, this time she was wearing a white gown and had a gold halo overhead, I asked her if she found Jesus, she said yes. I told her how happy I was for her, I asked if she had found out her name yet, she said no, that in Heaven no one has a name. Then as quickly as she had come she floated away. I thought that I would never see her again, but I was so happy for her. I was concerned because I didn't know if they had baptized her before she was buried.

I was convinced that I would never hear from her again. But one more time she appeared quickly, and said that I didn't have to worry about her. That she was with God. And that she would visit me from time to time. I thought where ever you go whatever you do, God is with you and your new home is heaven.

Now I realize that people say that all of this was just a dream. And that's what it was. But I really believe that baby came and communicated with me knowing that I would believe. The two of us were born the same month, the same year and she was identified as me. That will always give us a special bond. I know that she'll never be able to tell me who drowned her, because that's in God's hands. Most likely I'll never see her again.

The mother who raised me cherished this saying:

*"A hundred years from, now it will not matter what my bank account was, the sort of house I lived in or the kind of car I drove… But the world may be a different place because I was important in the life of a child."*

*—Forest E. Witcraft, Teacher, Scholar—*
*(1894-1967)*

Another passage my mother loved was this:

*"And a woman who held a babe against her bosom said: Speak to us of children, he said: Your children are not your children. They are the sons and daughters of life's longing to itself. They come through you but not from you, they belong not to you. You may give them your love but not your thoughts. For they have their own thoughts. You may house their bodies but not their souls, for their souls dwell in the house of tomorrow which you cannot visit even in your dreams. You may strive to be like them, but seek not to make them like you. For life goes backward nor tarries with yesterday. You are the bows from which your children as living arrows are sent forth."*

—*Kahlil Gibran, in* The Prophet—

I believe that my mother truly believed the above sayings and tried to raise me that way, with the church helping her out.

I sometimes still can't believe that all of the events of this book happened to me. But they did. Has it been easy to live with? NO. I would have preferred not knowing any of this. I was a very happy person before. My mother always told me that I was God's child. That is the one thing I clung to through all of this.

*Some people come into our lives and quickly go. Some stay for a while and leave footprints on our hearts.*
*And we are never the same.*

My wish for you is to sleep with angels!

# Acknowledgments

A thank you to Attorney Douglas M. Head, former Attorney General in Minnesota. It was Doug Head who first said to me that this story had to be told. He felt that it was part of the history of Minneapolis, and the State of Minnesota. Doug Head was not only a wonderful attorney, but a friend who truly cared.

Thanks to John R. Murphy, a former FBI Agent, retired and in private practice. Mr. Murphy exhibited that rare quality of dedication in his work. He told me in one of our meetings that of all the cases that he had worked on, my case was the best.

Tom Seifert, an attorney with Douglas M. Head, worked tirelessly on many aspects of this case. Without his tenacity, this book could not have been written.

I am grateful for the reporting in the Minneapolis Journal by a cub reporter named Eric Sevareid, who would become a CBS News commentator. I am also grateful to the Minneapolis Star and the Minneapolis Tribune for their in-depth reporting.

And thank you to Katie Clark Vecchio helped put this book together from another perspective.

# About the Author

Lorene currently lives in Seattle with her husband and high school sweetheart, Richard. They have two sons together, both of whom live nearby. Though she has roots in Wisconsin, Lorene considers herself a true West Coast person with a special affinity for Puget Sound and Mt. Rainier. Despite spending many years in Wisconsin, Lorene and family always find themselves drawn back to Seattle. As a sports fan, Lorene cheers for the Wisconsin Badgers and the Seattle Seahawks. She enjoys regular trips across I-90 to catch a football game at Camp Randall, or shop at the outdoor markets in Olympia.

Lorene firmly believes that it is God that gets you through the hard times of life. She and her husband are deeply involved in their church where he has served as a church elder and she sings and plays the organ. This is her first memoir.

CPSIA information can be obtained at www.ICGtesting.com
Printed in the USA
LVOW10s0227110614

389410LV00003B/3/P

9 780991 069934